SOMETHING SPECIAL

poetry **Pt** today

SOMETHING SPECIAL

Edited by Natalie Nightingale

First published in Great Britain in 2002 by Poetry
Today, an imprint of
Penhaligon Page Ltd, Remus House,Coltsfoot Drive,
Woodston, Peterborough. PE2 9JX

A Catalogue record for this book is available from the
British Library

ISBN 1 86226 715 4

Typesetting and layout, Penhaligon Page Ltd, England.
Printed and bound by Forward Press Ltd, England

Foreword

Something Special is a compilation of poetry, featuring some of our finest poets. This book gives an insight into the essence of modern living and deals with the reality of life today. We think we have created an anthology with a universal appeal.

There are many technical aspects to the writing of poetry and *Something Special* contains free verse and examples of more structured work from a wealth of talented poets.

Poetry is a coat of many colours. Today's poets write in a limitless array of styles: traditional rhyming poetry is as alive and kicking today as modern free verse. Language ranges from easily accessible to intricate and elusive.

Poems have a lot to offer in our fast-paced 'instant' world. Reading poems gives us an opportunity to sit back and explore ourselves and the world around us.

Contents

The Dandelion Clock

Standing tall, crowned with a delicate crochet globe,
I pluck from your green heart.
Tell me the time.
Downy seedlings united by the touching of outstretched
feathery headdresses.
Between my fingers I roll your succulent milky stem.
Tell me the time.
A fragile spherical cobweb, nature's timepiece.
A whisper, a breeze creates the opening of your aerial display.
Tell me the time.
A company of tulle clad dainty dancers pirouette excitedly.
I blow to release an unrehearsed presentation from
twirling ballerinas.
Now, tell me the time.

Mary Morley

Sonnet: Paeam To Persephone

The garden sparkles in the morning sun
Bedecked with dewdrop diamonds. Over the grass
Observe la small black shadow softly pass -
Persephone, intent on games and fun,
Goddess of spring, with copper-glinting fur,
Sipping fresh dew before it melts away
With the sun's strengthening; then stops to play
With fallen leaves, her senses all astir
For action; rolls and frisks in new-dug earth,
Sharpens her claws on smooth-barked lime tree's girth,
Leaps up the garden fence, holds herself steady;
Swift movement in the spindle-grass - a mouse?
She stiffens, then relaxes; from the house
Her mistress' voice announces: 'Dinner's ready!'

Charles Fowler

Spring Is Here

Wake up! Wake up!
Spring is here:
The storms have abated
Spring is celebrated.
Grass lively grows
In fields, on hedgerows
Spring is here, spring is here.
The dark days have gone
Brighter days have come.
Spring is here. Feel it,
It's joyous spring.
The flowers cheerfully declare it,
The birds gaily proclaim it.
Spring is here, spring is here.

Mary Frances Mooney

The Last Lap

Grandpa always assumes
folks like him best as he is.
And usually he's right.

He loves his birthdays: each one helps
to beat the odds by one more year.

The secret of ageing gently,
he says, is to accept with grace
whatever you can't fix.

Judgement Day he does not fear:
he's given more than taken.

He's only concerned
the end of his life should be
easy on us all.

He knows that death will come - and go.
Its time has the longest, loudest laugh.

    Roger Mather

Syracuse

And so we came to Syracuse and loved it most of all.
With silence shaped like holes in sound,
olive trees in older dust accuse no one, nor do they judge
'Fascisti' scrawled across a wall.

Down nine worn steps and thirteen years
vendettas rapped a dark brown door.
But we saw only sunlight, strained through haze.
The soft day's stillness drank the blackened shadows down
and cut a wound across the floor.

And in that silent room there waits
a grand piano with dusty keys
one sees the shaft of sunlight flee across the floor
in slow lament;
a dusky noon, a burning breeze. And so we came
and were content.

Peter Jones

Thoughts Of Home

Silver and chrome
Bring thoughts of home;
Rubbing and scrubbing,
Painting and daubing,
Knitting and sewing,
Digging and hoeing.

Oh! To go on holiday again
With the thousands off to Spain;
To lie and fry on sandy beach,
Ice cream and drinks within easy reach.

But wait! Why nurse these thoughts within the brain?
I prefer to stay in England with the rain!
Home is where the heart abides,
Not in theme park or coastal rides.
Home is where the roots go deep;
Where all the memories are there to reap.

We think of bygone days,
Of childhood ways,
Activities and friends.
Of school and war, make do and mend.
Long-term memory to the fore,
Tales to tell, repeat and bore.
A sign of 'age' past to recall,
Stories long and short and tall!

So, thoughts of home are dear to me -
Nowhere else I'd rather be!

Patricia Kennett

The Truth Of God

God gave us arms and hands,
And legs and feet - all to be used,
Each to fulfil its function.
He also gave us all a mind
To question, reason, and decide
Through how we feel
About His words.
That we may know and understand
Which of the 'sayings' that we read
Do come from God and not from man.
For evil men can lead astray
The gullible who do not think,
But accept all without a blink.
So use your own God-given mind;
Think for yourself!
And then decide
Which words are cruel,
And which are kind.

Brian Cunningham

A Special Person

A person came into my life
in time I took her as my wife,
it was so many years ago
how I remember, I don't know.

But it is written on my mind
and loving memories I find
of simple things that happened then
and seem to come to life again.

When I went for an interview
an office window I looked through,
and framed within I saw a face,
which through my life took pride of place.

It wasn't even in the spring
and yet my heart began to sing;
it was to be some time to wait
until at last I had a date.

Something was planted in my heart,
and here was love, right from the start,
and it stayed with us many years
with joy, accompanied by tears.

For Gwen, this lass, became my wife
and brought much happiness to life.
Fifty-eight years we had - and then
I was left on my own again.

But this, in life, will always be
our time is limited, you see,
when love, in memories, is there
you'll find that 'love is in the air'.

Laurence D Cooper

Emma And Phillip

May the promise you make,
As in reverence we all stand.
Remain with you forever,
When you exchange a golden band.
May the love you share,
Burn deep within your hearts.
And may your good sense,
Never let you drift apart.
For marriage is a partnership,
Each must play a part.
You both have love and honour,
There can be no better start.
Our fervent wish on this special day,
May our love go with you through life's way.

Tom Grocott

Crow's Song

Today the world is a garden,
A psychedelia of colour
With fantasies of fragrances.
The sun is warm on my cheeks,
The breeze soft in my hair
And I want to run and leap
To babble inconsequential joyous songs,
Though they might sound like
The anger of invaded crows.

How can these spring torrents
Course still, uncontrolled,
When I am too old to be undisciplined?

Could it be that you called to me
Cheerily from my garden,
Then came and kissed me
Where I sat?

Ted Harriott

The Iris

If I were a flower,
What would I be?
Tall and willowy with delicate petals
Vibrant colour and intense scent,
A picture of loveliness
To tempt passers-by with my beauty.
Swaying in the warm, summer breeze,
Will I be picked or stay in the sunlight?
Caressed by fine, summer rain
That heightens the senses
Rainbows dancing in the air,
Beacons of colour whose incandescence
Is only temporary, replaced
By a new contentment.

If I were a flower
What would I be?

Sarah Allison

Buddy

Buddy is my dream dog;
He has soft, golden hair.

He plays in the sunshine;
He doesn't have a care.

We walk him in the morning
We walk him in the night.

And every single day and night,
He makes my life seem bright.

Francesca Apichella (9)

My Best Friend

The unwashed bundle in my arms
Is the baby I have borne
Very tiny and so tender
Looking naked and forlorn.

As she grew her hair was curly
And her eyes a lovely blue
There were tears and little tantrums
But through all, our love was true.

We had trials and troubles
Our life was not all serene
But we were always together
And our sorrows were unseen.

Then when you and Roy were married
I missed you in my own way
I had my own love to help me
So we lived from day to day.

Now I'm alone, but still see you
I pray you never alter
You're my friend, I love you so
My dearest, lovely daughter.

Edith Buckeridge

Spring

High winds herald March in,
but spring is here in all its glory
still the same old story.
Everywhere I look I see the majesty,
the colours and sounds echo around.
My special time is here alone another year.
Memories still of lost love and what we had, make me sad.
But I must go on, accept what I have, try to be glad.
Hold in my heart the sight and sounds of Hannah's sweet voice,
when she says Nanny I love you, you're my bestest friend
my happiness knows no end, count my blessings,
care for my friends and marvel again at spring.

Maureen Andrews

Women Are So

You women are so able, yes
To perform many tasks at once
Making many men feel just like
Maybe they are the school dunce.

You women are so able, yes
To take on more and more
Making many men just look around
And just feel there is nothing left in store.

You women are so able, yes
To do most anything
Even now there is no difference
To the money either one can bring.

Keith L Powell

Lasting Love

From infant days the challenge great,
The surgeons all performed first rate;
Throughout the years our love just grew,
As daughter strove to challenges new.

At school the work was tough to take,
So many times her ears did ache;
But as we saw the effort made,
Our love just grew, there was no fade.

Exams just proved a touch too far,
Revision always caused some jars;
But sheer persistence drove her on,
Our love was there to shine upon.

In hospital she wore brave face,
To all the staff so full of grace;
Her hearing never reached the heights,
But bond of love grew ever tight.

The public tests were acts supreme,
Her struggles great, results a dream;
With help, support and love so great,
She got to college for teaching date.

Her children loved her help and care,
She knew their problems, some so rare;
In Dorset, Germany, Luton she taught,
Always so near with the love she sought.

Illness took over and steady decline,
Contact was closer, helpers were fine;
Love ever deeper as full time in bed,
Thank God for the memories stored in her head.

John Paulley

On Being Adopted

I'm sure I'm not the only one
        To offer you a home.
Some may have sought your pedigree
        In many a weighty tome.
Some may have tried beguiling you
        With well-intentioned word,
Only to see you turn your back
        As if you hadn't heard.
Sometimes you'd give a cautious sniff
        At would-be friendly finger,
Then make it plain it's waste of time
For such as they to linger.
You may be tabby, black or grey,
        You may be white as coley;
Somewhere, you're sure, a home awaits
        For you to conquer wholly.
So why did you make me your choice,
        Why honour me by choosing
My house and garden, food and fire,
        My bed to nurse your musing?
It's plain enough that I'm bewitched,
        But not so plain to see
Why you, of all the feline kind,
        Dear cat, decide on me?

Kathleen M Hatton

Remember

Remember the springtime,
Before dreams gone by,
The blue of the bluebells,
Matched up to the sky.
The grass where we sat,
Was the greenest of green,
The shy woodland primrose,
Tried not to be seen.

Remember the summer,
The walks on the shore,
When the warm Cornish sand,
Seemed to enter each pore.
With days that were lazy,
And nights long and warm,
The laughter when caught,
In a short, summer storm.

Remember the autumn,
All yellows and gold,
The smoke of the bonfire,
When stories unfold.
The food and the wine,
Were the essence of sharing,
The long moonlit walks,
When we knew about caring.

Remember the winter,
With snow on the bough,
The frost and the ice,
Brought a closeness somehow.
Those wonderful fires,
When the logs hiss and spit,
The coming of Advent,
When candles were lit.

T O Brookes

My Old Apple Tree

It's crooked now my apple tree
With branches old and dry
Where once its green leaves shaded me
I see now the clear blue sky
No apples grace its ancient boughs
Or blossoms fair and sweet
It seems together we've grown old
Our structures not so sleek
I have no heart to end it all
I would be cutting down a dream
Of happy days ad summer fun
Of tears and laughter in the sun
Now I just sit and think 'well done'
You've had a fruitful stay.

Dinah Sharman

Then Love Came

His name is Murphy, he came to me a year ago
Next to mine he fills the empty chair
And now I know I could never let him go.

He came when love had died and I was low
He asks for little and gives me a lot of care
His name is Murphy, he came to me a year ago!

Together we go for drives and walks we know
We don't say much, but our nearness is there.
And now I know I could never let him go!

He looks at me with eyes that glow
With love, and follows me everywhere
His name is Murphy, he came to me a year ago.

At games and hide and seek we often have a go,
He hides under the bed, I always find him there.
And now I know I could never let him go.

'Why do you love him so?' Ask people I know
He's my dog, a faithful companion for whom I care.
His name is Murphy; he came to me a year ago
And now I know I could never let him go.

Carolina Rosati-Jones

Steven

I remember you upon that special day.
Parade ground pomp, and ceremonial pride.
The beginning of your hard and chosen way.
The start of regimental life and much beside.

You in your air force blue, so proudly worn.
Grown from fresh-faced boy into a man;
And I thought back to the day when you were born.
That day when my pride in you began.

You have achieved so much, and through the years
Combined career and fatherhood within this span.
Faced single parenthood, determinably suppressed fears.
Proved once again you are a special man.

Proved yourself, time and time again.
Achieved and risen swiftly through the ranks.
Sought always to improve and have remained
A very special person, for whom we gratefully give thanks.

Jean Rosemary Regan

The Wedding Day

Hushed was the little church, the muted organ low,
The congregation waits, in the lamp's soft glow,
When suddenly fanfares ring loud,
Drowning the murmurs of the crowd.
Heads turn to view the bride, in radiant white,
The father proudly by her side, a lovely sight.
Whilst at the altar, standing fast,
The bridegroom waits his love at last.
Then so with stately walk, down the aisle she glides,
Bridesmaids sweetly on her train to reach his side.
The vicar there, his hand did raise,
To bid the people sing His praise.
Wilt thou then David, take this woman for thy wife,
To honour, love and cherish, all thy life?
And Karen too, response do'st give,
To love as long as ye both shall live.
The loving couple vowed with rings profound,
There in the sight of God to be ever bound,
Then down the aisle and out the door,
Husband and wife for evermore.

J Holloway

The Love That Surrounds Me

I am looking forward to seeing you
After such a long, long time
I have listened to your singing
I have felt your love on mine
Nurturing me from the beginning
Your heart beats so as mine
Giving life and love to me
I await for what will be
I have heard the many names
Both masculine and feminine
But you will not know for sure
Until the very time is due
When true love will ensue
The love that you will give to me
The love from me to both of you
Meanwhile I await the enter cue
When we will be on centre stage
For me to say my very first word
Mum and Dad I love you true
You're the best in all the world.

K K Campbell

Simply The Best

My beloved dog who's been with me for so many years,
First an ordinary puppy who selected me,
Determined that I'd fall in love with her, which I did,
Learning she was the 'runt' from the litter of twelve
So had to have vitamins for her growth from puppyhood.
When she assessed my disability we met head on.
She'd walk backwards to avoid upsetting me, tripping me!
Fetching clothes without difficulty, collecting what was dropped,
Even before she was trained by the DfD when she was two
After which her character changed - she became serious,
Staying with me, refusing walks unless I was there too,
Obeying all my orders and laying at my bad side, protecting me
Warning me who was at the door, sounding ferocious at strangers
But when they entered almost licking them all over, jumping for joy
Enduring the cats, even one who treated her as his mother!
Coming shopping with me, lying down in cafes, pubs or restaurants
So that nobody realised she was there, hidden under benches
She'd bring my post, waiting for the cats to finish their biscuits
Then clean the bed for me and if I spilt the milk licking it up.
Oh Skippy, my Skippy, an elegy is not enough, you were love
Unbound, unrestrained, shining through the most gorgeous eyes!

Tilla Smith

Dragonfly

From beneath the clear and sparkling stream
A larvae-like grub appears
Climbs up a leaf and sheds its skin
An insect emerges and like a dream.

Unfolds its crumpled wings to dry in the sun
Now its new life has just begun
A bejewelled acrobat and as time goes by
We now can see it's a dragonfly.

Blue and green like an emperor's crown
Hovering over the water up and down
Till it spies a lady same type as he
Says, 'Will you be my wife and marry me?'

So they dance in the sun, entwined together
While the sun beats down on the clear water
Bubbling and dazzling in the morning sun
Now their cycle of life has just begun.

Autumn rain now strikes the air
The stream is cold, no heat from the sun
New life's in the water for next year
But they lie on the weed their short life has gone.

Now your life is over
Regeneration, immortality and might
Jewelled emperor of the summer skies
Are now reflected in the pools of light.

Carol List

Shona

Your smile can lift my spirits high
Your kiss is soft as down
Your touch is gentle - almost shy
Your laughter halts a frown.

Your steps are quick and leave me tense
For caution plays no part
Your curiosity's immense
Your emotion's from the heart.

You crave attention all the time
And I'm impressed by what you do
Your very life is so sublime
- I can't believe you're only *two!*

Betty Nevell

Only A Dog!

'Only a dog!' They oft-times say
When comes the time, the parting-day.
Yet faithful to the end are you
No matter what we say or do.
When comes the day, you cannot stay.

A smile, sweet words, they were your pay
For love and loyalty every day.
Each day the bond between us grew
'Only a dog!'

Devotion when the day was grey,
Understood, when no words could I say,
My very thoughts you read, and knew,
Yet through my silence, devoted, true.
Who could with such trust repay?
'Only a dog!'

Joan Thompson

Tribute To Grandma

My grandma didn't wear a shawl
And sit about all day.
My grandma was so big and tall
She loved to sing and pray.
She told us all how Jesus died,
'For you and me,' she said,
I think the word was 'Crucified'
Upon a cross of wood.

My grandma told us of His love
And his care for us each day.
So as He lives in Heaven above
She taught us how to pray.
She told us just to speak to Him,
For He is right by our side,
He listens to our every word
And His arms are opened wide.

She told us how little children
Were taken to Him one day,
But as He was tired, the disciples
Tried to send them away.
But Jesus gently rebuked them,
Said, 'Let the little ones come unto me,'
So they all ran to Him gladly,
And some of them sat on His knee.

My grandma was always busy,
Helping the lonely and sad
Visiting the sick and the gloomy,
Making them happy and glad.
She loved us children dearly,
As only grandmas can.
As the years went by, she grew older,
So we called her dear old gran.

Now my grandma's gone to Heaven,
But I'll see her again some day.
She'll be right there with Jesus
Watching the angels play.
Then when they see me coming
The gates will open wide,
Then I'll hear the voice of Jesus
Say, 'Come child, right inside.'

E Squire

The Special One

Do you have time to think today
Perhaps about what you could say
To ease another's tragic pain
To help somebody to regain
Their strength and help them soldier on
Until they once again are strong
So that maybe they can cope
And look at life with bright, new hope?

You do? You are a special one
And you will find that you are drawn
To those who need a helping hand
A listening ear to understand
The world being full of dread and woe
Needs people such as you to sow
The seeds of happiness around
Even on the barren ground.

Where nothing it would seem will grow -
But you will try your best I know
How sad to think of people who
Do not have someone such as you
If I were in dire need at all
And on the edge - about to fall
How wonderful to have you there
If just to show another's care.

Norma Griffiths

Friendship

If you have a friend who is good and kind,
Treasure them through life, true friends are hard to find,
I once had a dear and sweet friend,
Nice in every way,
Always a smile upon her face,
To cheer you through the day,
She was kind to everyone, her heart was good and true,
Lord, please look after her now she is with you,
I will always remember her, she was one of their best,
But the Lord decided she must take a rest.

M Stevens

Ode To Our Sweet Daddy

Sweet saintly knight
Who's gone to rest
Guard over us
Who love you best.

Protect us now
And ever more
Until we meet
At Heaven's door.

We loved you well
We loved you ill
Then God's voice called
Your seat to fill.

Children old
And children young
A loving wife
Your praises sung.

God's gift of life
From parents both
He gave to you
To fill your troth.

You gave us life
You gave us love
Now Father dear
Guard from above.

Vivienne Rae Nolan

A Tribute To Chris

To a husband and dad we still dearly love,
Whom God has taken and now lives above.
At forty-six you were too young to die,
We miss you so much and wonder why.
You had to go and leave us behind,
Because we loved you so dearly, you were one of a kind.
When springtime comes and the blossom appears,
We think of the good times, the laughter, the tears.
Our love grew deeper as each year passed,
It was a love and affection that would always last.
You weren't only my husband, you were my best friend
So when flower buds open, this prayer we send.
God bless you and keep you, look down from above,
Remember our thoughts are of the one we love.
The day is now drawing fast to an end,
Goodnight, God bless, all our love we send.

Shirley Fordham

Smile Once More
(To Karen, Love Nan 17.11.1925 - 09.01.2002)

That I am not here
You may shed a tear
But in spirit I'll be
In the everyday things, that you see.

Do not despair
I am everywhere.
Whether it be the last star at night
Or dawn's first early light.

In time you'll see
You can smile once more
Then save one for me.

Angela Henderson

Wide Open Spaces

I love wide open spaces.
You can see for miles.
No mountains or hills
Animals grazing on the horizon
A sense of freedom
I can see everlasting ~
Life.

Noel Lawler

Beautiful Butterfly

Beautiful butterfly, balmy and bright,
sat on my toe in the warm sunlight.
The moment or two shared with me,
you showed me peace and tranquillity.

Perfectly balanced yet wild and free,
you came over and visited me.
A life so short but lived to the full,
your life cannot possibly be dull.

Graceful, inspiring, a delight to see,
your presence was felt all around me.
Totally captured in a serene glow,
there's no way you could ever be a foe.

When my mind is troubled I think of that day,
I was one with nature and you pointed the way.
Wings like an angel's, sensitive and strong,
the meaning of this message is to *soldier* on!

Kateryna Mazelan (nee Kozak)

A Special Man
(For Charles Stewart)

Lived with for a lifetime,
But I'd never really known
Until that day we said goodbye
Brought friends to whom he'd shown.

The gifts you give, can be simple ones
Of laughter, love and care
If you want to live forever
Then these are the gifts to share.

Was he a man of weaknesses?
No more than you or I
For the gifts he gave, were simple ones
That's why he'll never die.

Margaret Maud

From My Heart
(Dedicated to Karen)

From my heart I wholly adore you
And that's just the start
How I lived a life before you
I would barely take part.

Hand on heart I wholly implore you
That we should never part
Will not put anyone before you
So that we will never part.

I'd give you all that I promise
And that's just a fact
How I live now for only that one kiss
It is as simple as that.

Carve our names on a tree in a forest
My thoughts of you impart
Take a walk in the early morning mist
All my life . . . be my sweetheart.

Every morn I wake up beside you
Near takes my breath away
I hope you'll never bid me adieu
And in my arms will stay.

Lynn Thompson

We

We are the spirit,
We are the one,
We are the mercy,
We are the sun.

We are the beauty,
We are the birth,
We are the glory,
We are the Earth.

Death shall not defeat us,
No matter the cost,
Death shall not silence us,
Nor shall we be lost.

We are the cosmos,
We are the tower,
We are destiny's creatures,
We are the power.

Adversity shall not break us,
Whatever the pain,
Cruelty shall not consume us,
Nor evil reign.

We are the spirit,
We are the one,
We are the mercy,
We are the sun.

J Walker

Moment In Time

As a mere mortal
We can have a special moment
That only happens once
Like a million atoms
That merge as one,
As if the stars shine
Like great diamonds
Down on us
That one moment that we
Touch paradise.

June Sweeney

Norma

She was just seventeen when I first saw her
The year was nineteen fifty,
When fancy dance was all the rage
Jive and Bop they called it,
And it sorted out your age.
Her hair was short and auburn
It suited her that style,
And coupled with her antics
Had me gobsmacked for a while,
I watched her, confused with love and wonder
Just what should I do next?
I made a pass, but all I got
Was a look that said I'm vexed!
Then thankfully the music changed
A slow fox-trot, I think . . .
So like the gent I thought I was,
I asked her with a wink
To step upon the dance floor
And would she like a drink?
She looked at me with large, green eyes
And nodded her acceptance,
We slowly fox-trotted to the bar
And ordered gin and tonic,
And as we sat and started to talk
The mood was not platonic.
And so it was that in due course
The two of us were wedded,
And yes, of course, you've got it right
She was the dancing, little red head!

Bah Kaffir

A Well Loved Lady

There was a lovely lady, Elizabeth was her name,
Although she married the British king she never looked for fame,
Her manners were exemplary and she acknowledged rich or poor,
For a nicer Queen of England, you could not ask for more,
Her husband died which left the lady to cope on her own,
Until their daughter was ready to inherit the British crown,
The Queen Mother carried out lots of duties in the new
                                        queen's name,
Loving all her subjects and still treating them the same,
It seemed so incredible that the lady lived over one hundred years,
Much work she did in peacetime and through the world war years,
Never once did she falter or do anything that was wrong,
Well loved by lots of people through her whole life long,
No one can ever doubt that the lady always did her best,
So Lord, now her busy life is over, please give her eternal rest.

Stan Gilbert

Pen Friends In Love

I was a lonely man
I came from far across the sea
I found myself a pen friend
Her name was Beverley.
When I finally met her
I took her out to eat
We had a lovely time that night
She swept me off my feet.
Now she is my girlfriend
I love her through and through
I will love her till the day I die
My love for her is true.
I would like to marry her one day
I don't want to ever let her go
She's my little damsel
And I want everyone to know.
I was just an ordinary man
That was looking for romance
Now I'm her shining knight
A knight without a lance.

Stephen Hibbeler

The Queen Mum

Our lovely Queen Mum has passed away
Into the light of Eternal Day.
The memories she left span lots of years
And have brought laughter, joy and tears.

She enjoyed life and did her best
To cheer up those whose life lacked zest.
With a happy smile and twinkle in her eye
She would stop when others just passed by.

We are going to miss our precious Queen Mum
She loved her horses and watched them run
With Christian faith she worshipped the Lord
And believed in His Heavenly word.

So to our Queen Mum we say 'Farewell'
What the future holds we cannot tell
But we know that history will play a part
In the loss of a lady, dear to our heart.

Inez M Henson

Christmas

He who laid there,
Not a care in the world,
The most important man of all time,
The bearer of forgiveness,
The hand of faith,
The Son of God,
Was born,
Not crying not upset,
Just peaceful and wise,
Full of wisdom,
When He is older He will be great,
The man who defied the hatred in the world,
This man gave us forgiveness like no other,
He was the miracle maker,
Who gave up His life for all mankind,
He was not born a king,
But in a stable,
His followers worshipped Him,
And He worshipped His Father,
The Holy Spirit.

Camilla Davidge

Dedicated To My Dad

I've never had my mother
I've always had you Dad
You brought me up
And cared for me
And told me off when bad.

We've made it through the bad times
And through the good times too
If Dad you ever left me
I don't know what I'd do.

Nothing can come between us
Me, my dad, and I
Not until the world's to end
Till darkness clouds the skies.

I'm so proud of what we've got
It's something special
It's something true
And I found a way to let you know
To write this poem for you.

Zoe Traynor

Uncle Jimmy

Old photos on my bedroom floor
Hurt my heart and make it sore
Reminding me of days now gone
Happy times, a special song
Crisp, white shirt, smartly dressed
It's true he only takes the best
For you were surely that to me
There can never ever be
Another one to take your place
To step inside that smiling face
To have a heart as kind can be
A soul as deep as any sea
Unique you were in every way
And even now I hear you say
'Hello my darlin',' just once more
As you greet me at the door
And it's with pride I write this down
For even now you're still around
Forever there inside my soul
And time they say will heal this hole
That you have left in all our lives
For you'll live on while we survive
To watch us now, as we grow old
Relaying stories you once told
And knowing that as time goes by
Your photos will not make me cry
Instead I'll smile as I recall
The loveliest uncle of them all
Who'll promise me whatever my fate
He'll meet me there at Heaven's gate.

Lesley Hartley

The Old Pit

The pithead wheel is silent now,
for the final shift is done,
and the ragwort blooms in profusion,
at last light of the sun.

Daggers of glass in broken windows
- shine, an autumn moon in the eastern sky,
a broken door swings to the breeze,
and the wild swans homeward fly!

This place of haunted shadows
of a million bitter tears,
a dark, forgotten tombstone
of dreadful, toiling years!

A Teesdale

The New Shoes

I was having a wonderful day
Stripped to the waist, and the bands did play
The wine was flowing, I couldn't lose
Until somebody stole my shoes.

I took them off to crack my toes
I looked around at well . . . who knows
When I turned back they were gone
I thought it was a joke, what was going on?

A pair of cat boots that I'd just bought
For seventy quid, someone's got the lot
I'll never look at people the same
Where's my boots, is that them?

My day was spoiled, so I told the guard
Bare chest and shoeless
He said, 'You think you're hard.'
Louder and louder I did protest
They turfed me out, you might have guessed.

So there I am standing outside looking in
The bouncer on the gate cross-armed with a grin
The band on stage just a distant din
In frustration and anger I kick a bin
Then hop around screaming
With my toe caved in.

So the next time you go shoe stealing
Remember how it left me feeling
In my stocking feet I limped up for the train
When I got off at the station
It had started to rain.

J Baird

My Special Day

I had reached the age of 60,
nothing remarkable in that.
But my wonderful family
soon changed all that.

There were cards to open
and little presents too.
It's a special day, they said,
what shall we do?

We looked round the shops
and as if on a hunch,
my sister suggested
we stay out for lunch.

I thought it looked
quite a posh place
and, indeed
that was the case.

We walked in the door
to a wonderful scene.
There were all the family
that day, I hadn't seen.

There was laughter and tears
as the meal progressed.
What a wonderful family,
I felt I was blessed.

Julie Brown

Sunset Over Solway Firth

The falling sun sheds rays of light,
Upon the water twinkling bright;
The tide receding from the shore,
The children digging, for bait to store.

The sparkling pools of brilliant light,
Create a circle, so brilliant, bright;
The limpets on the rocks stick fast,
But locals collect them, first and last.

The ever-darkening clouds now rise,
As sun descends and birds grow wise;
They gather in their flocks to feed,
From tide which brings both food and reeds.

That brilliant red reflects o'er hills,
As sun now drops and sea is still;
The rocks all dark with seaweed cover,
The late night calls of black billed lovers.

A glorious coastline, clear but dark,
Its silhouette is now so stark;
To sit and gaze on Solway Firth,
Brings thoughts and dreams of native birth.

John Paulley

51

My Shaded Niche

The glorious sun in all its warmth
Hangs above me like a peach,
So I laze in shaded corners
Where its ripeness cannot reach.

Mid morning finds me by the pond
Where a figure stands in lead,
And water reflects upon the ivy
That climbs an old potting shed.

Under the apricot tree on a slatted bench
Come twelve o'clock I lay,
Falling nicely into pleasant dreams
To the sound of the fountain spray.

Mid afternoon I sit myself
On a circle of London stocks,
Which I share with a table and chair
And thirsty plants in pots.

From upon my seat I lift my head
To wisteria that gently towers,
Then my attention's drawn to a busy bee
That disturbs a bed of flowers.

Now as evening falls a darken cloak
Has wrapped around the sun,
And my shaded niche has become
A place where spiders' webs are spun.

So I pass the ferns and take the path
That edges round the lawn,
I'll say goodnight to my shady niche
I'll be back tomorrow morn.

Peter J McBride

Our Eden

Thank God for the joy of a garden,
The wonder of growing things,
As the bud bursts into a flower
With the beauty that it brings.

Snow lays deep in the garden,
And all seems dead and bare.
But the earth is only sleeping,
Safe in the Father's care.

Spring will come to the garden,
A miracle then we'll see,
Here a bulb appearing,
There a leaf on a tree.

How much in life would be missing
If we were not to know
The privilege of working
In God's garden here below?

Amelia Wilson

A Special Person

How quickly the gripping tendrils of despair
Sweep through that weakened body with delight,
And now searching out those undefended parts
Absorbing them with ever-quickening fright.

Thoughts must be there, but then movement does not come,
As if a block of stone is now in place
Just awaiting a miracle of release,
To quicken now a weakened, fumbling pace.

Thoughts now searching out intending paths to take,
As to and fro they're changing constantly,
Now at last the battle seemingly in place.
There are no clues, who will the winner be?

But those clutching hands that torture all before
Creating fear with such a great delight,
Gripping fiercely every nerve it searches out
Tries to evoke the desperate need to fight.

And so now the body slowly makes its move
Determined to take on the weary fight,
Each step now a mounting hurdle but to climb,
The shaking body steels itself with might.

Progress is so slow and very cumbersome,
Willingness to survive is there indeed,
Bringing out that hidden depth of strength inside,
That can be harnessed, with hope, to succeed.

Finally, slowly, the struggle dying down
Movement takes on its role, a job well done,
And contentment showing on the countenance,
Battle is not lost, but so bravely won.

Irene Grahame

Love From A Sunday Morning

We used to walk up to Glusburn Gib
And sit there on the grass
We used to watch the cows and sheep
And distant traffic pass.

Young lovers with our earnest dreams
We spoke of a future planned
Warm in the rays of the morning sun
A sparkling diamond on my hand.

A strong arm around my shoulders
Our two minds completely in tune
His smiling, blue eyes and sweet, warm breath
As he promised me even the moon.

And then back we'd go to Sunday lunch
A feast simply like no other
There was never a Yorkshire pudding
To compare with those of his mother.

Is it really forty years since then?
Today our third daughter moves on
Alone but together, we think of the plans
And where all the years have gone.

Ann Marriott

Movie Classics

Going, going, Gone With The Wind:
Now Rhett, he didn't give a damn
And left poor Scarlett in a jam.
Well hush ma mouth, ah loves da south!

Shane is the mysterious stranger:
He's fast as lightning on the draw,
The fastest Joey ever saw.
But rides off alone - his name echoing.

Fearless Flynn fights for freedom:
Sir Guy is rotten to the core
And very soon he'll be no more,
Thanks to the great and good, Robin Hood!

Mitchum's a psychotic preacher:
His hands are tattooed L-O-V-E and H-A-T-E,
So what will be the children's fate?
The money's hid in the rag doll!

Swanson, swanning around on Sunset:
Her pictures really did get small
And now she's waiting for the call
From her director, Mister De Mille.

Basil and the Baskervilles:
For Holmes and Watson the game's afoot
And clues together they must put,
To solve the case of the 'devil' hound.

A towering Citizen Welles:
Death is near for Charles Foster Kane
And wishes he was a child again.
Where . . . is . . . Rosebud?

Cavan Magner

Idle Thoughts From The Bottom Of The Garden

The year passes. Late afternoon. The sun's rays
slant across the roughly-laid stones of the patio.
Hollyhocks by the pool's side, lit by the blaze,
are in a dapple of palest yellow
set against darkest red.

The day goes and the water lilies close
while overhead spears, dark and light green,
of a tropical sisal plant screen a tottering greenhouse
where a vine, oh slowly, through a broken pane bears
promise - is it? - of what the year may bring in grapes.

And the panorama abides, though Old Man's Beard
cascades over the tangle within of bikes, ragged card tables,
wood, the year's accumulation of 'let's keep'.
Could one see ahead little would be changed,
save the pond; the heron emptied all twenty-five of our
flourishing fish. I simply know, come the summer's end,
my beloved will have rehoused and placed netted cover over
them against such predatory appetite in a safer residence
for them close to the house.
And I, for whom the bird was a bookmark framed
in many a happy memory, will banish it into a dark
other than that in which it plundered.
And you, my love, and I, we will rejoice in the year's laughter.
After all, delight and song are strung
brightly, along our way.

   John K Coleridge

Hynes

Like a rock he stands
The cliff edge stands facing the force of the sea
The water is not always the same
Yet it feels it is often stormy
One day the water is calm
Yet the rock still stands forceful
He is shouting and standing, claiming his land
Not surrendering
But the water is calm
He does not listen!
The sea feels angry, but this sea will never attack
She leaves, but takes her anger away
The cliff edge still stands
The sea returns, but does not scream
She stays longer this time
Still the cliff edge stands strong, hard, protective
He has no time for the sea
The sea feels angry and swirls away
Yet still she can see the cliff edge and she cannot ignore him.
The sea hears his yell and feels calm no more
The land darkens
She comes ever forceful, crashing directly into the cliff
The cliff silences. He welcomes the sea. And she stops.
The storm stops. It is a calm night.
Side by side they watch the night sky.
By morning there is a cave, an opening in the cliff edge
The water rides through, to the side of the land she likes
She settles within the cavern. Safe, secure, welcome
And the cliff edge screams no more.

Hayley Paget

Young Private Unwin

No vast marble cross marks Private Unwin's grave,
no giant stone angel signs his last rest and slumber:
just monuments to the rich overshadowing the brave.

No grand epitaph testifies to what young Unwin gave,
too young to fight, too young for name and number:
no vast, marble cross marks Private Unwin's grave.

No Union Jack proudly flies to and fro in the wave,
recalling bloody trench, and cannons unbroken thunder:
just monuments to the rich overshadowing the brave.

No consoling words of valour, to treasure and save,
what of the fallen, those slain in battle and blunder:
no vast marble cross marks Private Unwin's grave.

No Essex flowers to garnish his graveside shade,
where that English heaven, to behold and wonder:
just monuments to the rich overshadowing the brave.

No epilogue for this young soldier that England made,
eclipsed by powerful merchant, and wealthy monger:
no vast marble cross marks Private Unwin's grave,
just monuments to the rich overshadowing the brave.

Keith Leese

A Special Grandma

I had a special Grandma
At 16 Tyndale Street.
I used to like to visit her
And play around her feet.
She always wore black dresses
That reached down to the floor;
I thought she must be very old
When I was only four.
She had a picture on the wall
Of ducks beside a mill
And she would give me toffees
And I can taste them still.
She still retained her gaslights,
Which gave a bright white light,
And had a hanging chain pull
To turn them off at night.
Her home had green linoleum
On front and back room floors
And wallpaper with flowers
And varnished, panelled doors.
I loved that dear old lady,
Who was always kind to me,
And always had some buttered scones
When we went round for tea.
I never heard her say a word
That wasn't warm and kind;
She always had a smile although
Her face was deeply lined.
She left us many years ago
But often I recall
The house at 16 Tyndale Street
With flowers on the wall.

D A Calow

Magical Moments

Magical moments of a dream come true,
excitement of the show - and the crowd it drew.
Anticipation as time draws near,
for the curtain to go up and the cast to appear.
The orchestra plays, it accompanies the show
and the audience applaud as the crescendo does grow.
The theatre is lit softly by lights here and there,
each spectator sitting alert in their chair.
Row after row involved with the theme,
some wishing it was them in the theatrical scene.
An evening like this helps problems fade away,
of course you know they will return next day.
But tonight is for make-believe for just letting go,
giving way to emotion and enjoying the show.

B Lamus

Heavenly Hill

My head inches over the vertical green
To a velvet green plateau and blue sky scene
A constant cool wind drops exertion red heat
Twice being denied on the third this hill's beat.

Skylark and wind combine to caress
Tapping into my senses and draining duress
Precisely placed paces to turn half around
The main feature view that releases no sound.

Hungry eyes feast on this flat valley's delights
Aerial Movietone News views from this hill's heights
Blue vein rivers run round green patchwork fields
Mini tractors white spraying to increase crop yields.

Polluting plume rises from power plant's spout
It rises to Heaven before fading out
Grey arteries run from grey village to town
The old woollen mill stands out in brick brown.

Eye lenses capture deep into my mind
Pure, potent photos to eternally find
Closing the shutters as hunger's full fed
The bright sun shines through, yellow, orange and red.

A low, lean back angle into the breeze
Outstretching my arms launches linear time freeze
This moment clears cobwebs and anchor chain cares
I escalate skywards to rare angel airs.

Perfect peace breathes and then warmly grows
Filling me all from my head to ten toes
Ethereal experience slow motion dream
Swimming in oil translucent and clean.

Skylark and wind with their wrap-around sound
Pop the time bubble I glide to the ground
Descending to earth from this heavenly high
A teardrop escapes from the stars in my eye.

Andrew Younger

The Woman

I saw her shuffling up the street
worn-out shoes on her weary feet
her head was bowed against the wind
a more lonesome sight would be hard to find.

She carried a tattered canvas bag
her coat no more than a shabby rag
her back was bent against the snow
and she shuffled along at a pace so slow.

I took her arm as she crossed the road
and tried to relieve her of her load
but her hand gripped tight the canvas bag
though its weight alone made her body sag.

I led her safe to the other side
she squeezed my hand as I tried to hide
the tears that filled my eyes just then
and I started to pray to the Lord again.

'Please help her Lord, for she is old
bent of body with hands so cold
underneath her heart is warm
completely hidden by her wizened form
she needs your love to face each day
until such time as she's called away.'

I turned to see her disappear
and wiped away a falling tear
so many folk in the world today
are cold and hungry, old and grey
but if each of us could play a part
and bring some joy to an aching heart
then our lives would not be in vain
and humanity would smile again.

Diane Ingram

Memories Of Home

How much I enjoy walking
In the footsteps of Wordsworth and Coleridge.
Amongst the fells,
Along the lakes
Where golden daffodils bloom.

To walk to Borrowdale,
Staring at the Bowder Stone.
Looking over to Nitting Hawse -
Which bring back memories
Of a climb, still I recall.
As I take on Catbells
On such a hot, sunny day;
Admiring the beautiful scenery -
My eyes transfix towards Skiddaw
And its snow-covered top.
I descend from High Spy
Amongst the heather and the bracken.
The quiet of such tranquillity
Is pierced by the sound of running water.
As I reach the village of Grange -
Crossing over its two bridges
And back to Keswick I go
To write my memories down.
Not that I shall ever forget them -
So deeply impregnated in my mind
And in my heart and soul.

For just being a Lakeland poet
There is no place more special than home.

Anthony Clarke

Prelude To The Afternoon Of A Fawn
By Debussy

Dreamy, reminiscent of *Bambi*, this piece of music;
Just listen, you can picture the baby deer waking up;
Big, brown eyes wide with wonder at his surroundings.
Looking round, getting up slowly, unsteadily, spindly legs unfolding
From underneath a brown, velvet body.
Nuzzling up to his mother, shy, unsure, looking for comfort.

Then finding his feet, he leaps and bounds with playful energy,
Joining the others in fun and frolics, his white scut flashing,
Legs kicking, big pointed ears rotating to new sounds;
Long, pointed face leading the way,
Taking everything in.

Then quiet again, serene, as evening falls and the fawn grows weary;
He nestles up to his mother again and suckles,
Taking in a long, long draught of warm milk.
Soothing, nourishing, creamy, trickling down his slender throat,
Sending him into a long sleep; dreaming of grass, buttercups,
Bluebells and trees.

Kathy Rawstron

What's Special?

What's special?
Is it yes or no to special,
Is it success?
Is it birth?
Is it death?
Is it happiness or sadness?
Is it wedding,
Or desire dream having?
Is it love?
Al these
And others,
Or one, or many!
Are special to many,
But to have special,
To choose one special,
That's one over other specials.
I choose love,
It's the great desire love,
To kiss my beloved,
To enjoy love,
To share life,
To be happy with love,
That's the best special,
The over all specials.

Jalil Kasto

Something Special

Someone known to me
How desirable yet can someone
Be known
Seed sown grown still changes
How much more someone
All almost hourly, certainly daily
Pass through ranges of changes
Like money changing hands or
Credit cards swiftly effecting the deal
Until finally the purse is empty
The pocket light items purchased gone
Someone known to me loved treasured
Now passed in the exchange to the other side
Still pockets of light in the memory reside.

Bella Carroll

Man In A Raincoat

Rounding the bookshelves
from Mind, Body and Spirit,
I saw him, the boy they called
The Trainspotter.

Eyes locked, decades rolled back,
and the dull, grey man in the raincoat
gave way to a tall young man with glasses,
neat, quiet spoken, shy with girls,
whose friends were always somewhere else.

I rescued him, sheltered him, healed him -
he was my brother, best friend, lover.
Across his blank pages I scrawled
my future hero, my Prince Charming.
I loved him, I adored him, idolised his anorak.

Yearning for a love story,
I tried to analyse the plot.
But it was hidden in a language
only he could understand,
and he was writing a different book.

I left the shop, not looking back
at the dull, grey man in a raincoat,
seedy, odd-looking, slightly suspect.
Time had not been good to him -
the saggy skin, the baggy eyes,
spoke of early promise unfulfilled.

Perhaps I was mistaken.
All I really saw was a dull grey man in a raincoat
perusing the Transport Section in a book shop,
who caught my eye for a wink in time.
Yet the memory lingers on.
                    How did he see me?

Sue Murray

69

Love At First Sight

She is walking on sunshine,
On the sunny side of the street.
As she steps over the cracks -
The dust is gold beneath her feet.

From head to toe in beauty,
And all that women admire.
Dancing butterfly beyond reach,
She is all that men desire.

As she looks up to the sky,
I hope our gaze will someday meet.
Her presence is like fine perfume,
A whiff - then the allure's discreet.

Reading beyond the front cover,
Beneath that endearing smile.
There's something in the way she moves,
You know the woman has got style.

Stepping in and out of my dream,
Her body shimmers in the heat -
She is walking on sunshine,
On the sunny side of the street.

Olliver Charles

Not One, But Many

A baby's first cry,
First smile,
First step,
The first ray of dawn
As it chases long, dark shadows.
The first golden sunrise climbing high in the sky,
The rainbow of promise its colours stand bright
Its start and its finish disappear from sight.
The dawn's chorus heralds a new day
The sweet smell of freshly cut hay,
The first snowdrop, bluebell, daffodil, rose.
New-born lambs stand on thin, shaky legs
Bleating and nudging mums to be fed.
New life, new growth,
Sweet summer rain.
A sunset of fire has to be seen
For you cannot describe how it makes you feel
Its beauty and serenity, oh so very real.
Walks in the moonlight with your love by your side,
Picnics by the river with your child.
The end of summer when autumn stands at your door
Leaving golden carpets for you to admire.
The first snowflakes of winter,
Jack Frost plays his games,
Patterns on windows
White laced gowned trees.
So many special times go unnoticed,
So many special times we don't see,
Maybe if we stood awhile,
Maybe then, could we?

Mary Neill

The Birth Of My Children

All six were welcomed,
Each one a miracle of nature.
One born in Dorset, one in Devon
The other four in Hampshire, each one a gift from Heaven.

Mum and Dad searched for all fingers and toes,
Each one kissed on its little button nose.
We walked tall whether daughter or son
Proud to walk out with each one.

Life was hard, washing boiled outside in fire-fuelled coppers
Hard up and happy, we protested to the knockers,
It was our choice, having waited years,
Although now and again, tiredness and tears.

I am glad I had them in the years I did
Life was simple, good and kind, from nothing hid.
Now all six are grown with children of their own,
Washing machines, disposable nappies and dryers they all own.

Life now, one has had to learn
Is very different from those simple days
Not just out to play with a kiss
Now these days one has to mind,
That from the gate there are no strays.

Each one a blessing from God above,
Bringing with them family, harmony and love.
If life I had to live again,
From having children, I would not abstain!

Kathleen Collins

Moments
(For Rob)

Magic Moments of your life,
Beyond all reason, beyond all strife,
These are the jewels in the crown
To most remember when you're down.

Brandenburg Number 5
Bach's eloquence, it's full of life;
The hurtling sonata Prokoviev's 7
This is the great soloist's heaven;
Sharing this with a friend that's true,
It's one of life's mysteries that sees you through.

The dark countryside with the vast sky above,
Where I once felt the power of God's love;
The friendship circle that could be so great
Enveloped in your inevitable fate.

So we remember the beauty involved
Peace was its message, around it revolved
The people who came into our lives;
We accept all this with appreciative sighs.

It's more than nostalgia in this rhyme,
To remember those Magic Moments in time.

John D Williams

73

A Very Special Invitation

Oh the excitement and the joy that was in our hearts,
The day we received a very special invitation.
From the Lord Chamberlain, for the Queen.
The royal coat of arms stamped on the back.

To the front was the Buckingham Palace postmark,
Which from all the other letters, it had been set apart.
Was this really happening to a couple such as us?
Were we really the rightful recipients of this example
Of the calligrapher's art?

We opened the envelope so carefully
So as not to damage the contents within.
We could hardly contain ourselves
Our heads were in a spin.

So this very special invitation was before us
Upon it was the crown
ER and the copperplate embossed in gold.
Several times between us it was read,
In excitement and in doubt
Could this really be what it said?

The Lord Chamberlain is commanded by Her Majesty
To invite
Mr and Mrs Roger Young
To a Garden Party
At Buckingham Palace
On Thursday 15th July, 1999 from 4-6pm

An invitation we could not turn down
Lest we make Her Majesty frown.

Fiona E Young

A Special Person

It's many years since 'one of few'
Became my aid:
And gradually the friendship grew -
A seal was made.

Time passed - she married, moved away.
We had our views,
And came her card each Christmas Day
With all her news.

But now I'm old, alone and fear
We'll never meet,
But still her message comes to cheer
And friend to greet!

Ruth Shallard

The Promise

The sunshine glinted from your hair,
You looked so happy, not a care.
The day was ours, it felt so good,
I felt your love, I always could.

We stood together, side by side,
Forever now your steps I'd guide.
Upon your finger I placed the ring,
And then the choir began to sing.

They sang of a pair who were soon to be one.
They sang of a love that outshone the sun.
The birds fell silent as the music rose high,
The wind that had been blowing reduced to a sigh.

We walked from the church as a man and his wife
Our first day together for the rest of our life.
Our love it will carry us all the way through,
Since I said those two magical words. *I do.*

Neil A Forrester

The Lost Weekend

I had such a good time
With all my friends around me.
But now I'm back here
In a giant hole in the universe
Thinking only,
About my lost weekend.

The more I talk about it
The more distant it gets
I wish it could always be like that
But I know it would never be the same
I'll just have to think
About my lost weekend.

I wish I was still there
It could never be as bad as this
It seemed less cold there
Sitting here I realise what a dump this place is
And reminisce about
The lost weekend.

Gemma Stothard

Moments

I stop what I'm doing, to listen to the birds
Singing, making their nests. Spring's in the air
Looking up, a rainbow shining in warm, shimmering rain
A feeling I may add, you cannot explain.
Blossom pink, apple-white, fill the trees just in sight.
Lambs that dance across a field
Playing with pals they take no heed
To Mum who bleats don't go too far,
A broken fence, a speeding car.
Special moments are when you stop,
Take in, savour, maybe wonder
Sometimes answers, sometimes not
Just left with the moment
Maybe quietly ponder
A moment in time
That moment is mine,
Like first love, there are not words, you feel the moment
Etched in your mind, for years to come
Was the love, was my life,
My only one.

Maureen Watts

Calm Of The Moon

Young years ago you dumped me
when your sun was rising
and my shadow had to shrink.

You were journeying on a clearway to the light.
I was hunting dreams; his hand was warm and firm.
I was a spare part that had to go.

Now my ship has come down sky lanes,
becalmed on the edge of moonstorm
and from your cache of memories you cannot know

that I had planted cherry trees, the fruit is ripe,
the stones are scattered over fields
to root and blossom on my journey home.

You do not speak, but both of us regret
the blackthorn at the holy city's gate.
Your eyes have filled with tears.

John H Hope

My First Dance

Sometime around the year 1934 while in the CCC
(Civilian Conservation Corps) I attended my first dance.
I had never been to a real dance and danced with a girl.
Not only me, but several other guys in the camp
were in the same boat, so we got together and practised
dancing with one another.

The dance was coming up and we made an agreement
that if we didn't dance with a girl that night
we would have to run through a belt line the next day.
The belt line was a double line of boys with their belts in
their hands, who would take a whack at you as you ran through.
I had no intention of doing that.

So on the night of the dance I stood on the sideline
with a mouth full of chewing gum, chewing it a mile a minute
to ease my nervousness.
One of the boys ahead of me had his face slapped on his first try.

I figured if I had to go, go first class so I picked out a girl with
long, beautiful, black hair and I broke in on her.
I probably had a wrestler's hold on her while still chewing,
when suddenly I noticed a strange taste in my mouth.
My chewing gum was caught in her hair!
I immediately stopped chewing and continued dancing
with locked jaws, hoping someone would break on me.
When they finally did I opened my mouth, backed off
and hit the door. I never saw her again.
I eventually became a fairly good dancer and came to enjoy it
over the years.

Life is full of problems but you just have to 'stick to it'.

Frank Davis

Dreams Can Come True

The night is set on fire with cameras flashing
The atmosphere is completely amazing
Bodyguards make a safe path for the stars
As they step out of their big fancy cars

Julia! Tom! Mel! Brad!
My name isn't called but I really don't care
Like a child I just stand and stare
There's no other word to describe how I feel
It's simply *'surreal'*

What they wear doesn't depend on the weather
It can be anything from glitter, silk, suede or leather
People aren't here to make small talk
They're here to turn heads on the world's biggest catwalk.

My hand is taken and gently kissed
I can't believe I wasn't missed
My heart leaps around my chest
My breathing becomes heavy - I must have a rest

I turn to the crowd and a camera flashes
I feel the tears touch my lashes
My moment is here
The one I've dreamt of each and every year

Dreams can come true . . .

Carol Moore

There Are None so Blind . . .

Early dusk:
The sun sank slow behind the mountain ridge
And the sky turned a fiery orange-red.
The snow field, high against that glowing glory,
Did not reflect, but took upon itself
The complementary colour to the red
A clear, pale, lucid emeraldic green.

'Look!' I called 'Up there! See the green snow!'

My companion did not turn, he did not look,
But answered flat: 'Snow isn't green, it's white.'

So I looked upward to the ridge and watched
The orange fade, green become foggy grey.

For perhaps two minutes nature worked her magic,
Then drew the curtain of the coming night
And sank back into *'commonplace'* again.

F Jones

Golden Wedding

We weathered the hot Saturday July afternoon
Celebrating a very special occasion of a Golden Wedding couple
A ring, symbolic for love, true marriage
Often blessed for couples and the children
Discussing peace in spacious room
These times were then revealed.

Antidotes were said by friends
And the couple's precious memories are a wonder of fulfilment
As golden lengthy day cherished among the loving dreams
So many good friends have come to celebrate this special day
It's such a comfort to know this glorious beauty is shared
                                                    with closeness
We won't forget this wonderful get-together for being there
                                            in perfect harmony.

Heather Aspinall

Long Ago

The air is still, the heat of the day has gone
Rippling waters reflect lights from houses and
I can smell flowers and coffee
and hear sounds of music in a cafe bar,
as I wander along with thoughts of you
and think of the things we used to do.

Yes, we walked this way, we kissed and listened
as the clock chimed in the square and knew this
was the start of our love affair.

Life was lovely with not a care -
we had the rest of our lives to share,
but not everything in life is fair, no one knows
just when or where the happiness one has,
is snatched away, and you are left to face another day.

Heather Moore

Child's Play

Those happy carefree days
On common land we met to play;
Amongst the trees, beside the pond
Fishing for tiddlers with rod and string.

Daisy chains adorned our necks;
The sun shone down to warm our toes.
We spent long hours
Those summer hours, in sweet content,
And then to bed we went.

Sheila Macmillan

Treasured Memories
(For Elle, Nanny Carol and Grampa Wilf)

You are only three years old
A girl so sweet and small.
You ask so many questions
And think I know it all.
I can answer some of them
About this world of ours,
I can teach you all the names
Of animals and flowers.

But you have other questions
And I don't know what to say;
You ask where your great-grandad is
And why he's gone away.

I tell you he's in Heaven
And we can't visit there.
I know you think about him
When you sit in his old chair.
But although he's far away
Sometimes he's nearby too,
As a Guardian Angel
He's watching over you.

Although we cannot see him
In Heaven, high above
He'll always be here in our hearts
And we'll still have his love.

Pamela Evans

A Violin's Cry

He who makes the violin sing
pulls at my heart strings.
From frisky songs
to aching melodies
that stir mixed memories,
he glides from string to string
whilst provoking weeping and wailing.
Moving from pizzicato to languorous tunes
he transports my soul to tears of joy
or rapturous bliss,
like a small kiss placed gently upon
your forehead on a summery evening
visited by fireflies that twinkle
in the soft, blue, velvety night.
Hold on to the strains of that one
last note, taking care not to
let it slip through your fragile
fingers like sifting sand, hold on . . .

Myra Rigor Selvadurai

A Special Moment With My Father

There were so many things
I had meant to say
So many feelings
I meant to convey
But as you slept
In the hospital bed
Weary with life,
The full life you'd led
I sat by the window,
By your side
Watching fields of barley
Waving golden outside.

There was no need to say
Things meant to be said
No need to convey
The feelings inbred
Only be there
By your side
Watching fields of barley
Waving golden outside.

Geoff Sumner

Simply The Best

The song was played over and over
More times than the White Cliffs of Dover
In the times she has seen, and in times oh so lean
We all sang the tune of 'God Save The Queen'

As long as most people remember
From January through to December
Through all of the years, and all of the tears
When the King and his Queen, assuaged all our fears

The Blitz, it could never deter them
The rubble brought tears, she would share them
The King and his Queen, were there to be seen
Most of this century, so calm and serene

On the loss of a spouse, Oh so early
In a life with the 'Kings and Queens Pearly'
From Barnet to Bow and much further you know
She was Queen and a Mother to upstairs and below

The century treated her gently
Her transport, a Rolls, not a Bentley
Wherever she went, people's necks were bent
To just catch a glimpse of the Queen Mum, as she went

Sandringham, Windsor, Balmoral or where
She held her head high, even rejected a chair
But when the time came and God crooked his finger
As she'd done all her life, the Queen didn't linger

So in 2002 with millions in view
The hearse drove to Windsor, tears shed, old and new
So now there she lies in her favourite house
Lying with daughter and long gone spouse.

Tommy Glynn

A Christmas Message

News of new life
As Christmas draws near
To Angela and Chris
A baby next year

Hope for the future
A baby will bring
The beauty of summer
New life of the spring

Joy for our family
A new one to cheer
With joy and love forever
As new birth draws near.

As Mary gave birth
To our Saviour and King
May happiness and mirth
Greet this child with a grin.

William Dyer

Bedroom Mirror Rock Star

From eyes screwed tight, singing ballads
into a roll-on deodorant and picturing Wembley-heaven;
to me and Gavin, in Slimmy's lounge,
rocking on pool cue/lead guitar,
with Iron Maiden turned right up to eleven.

From rehearsals in the garage -
sunglasses on, whilst your brother
moved from one to another with his pocket torch/spotlight;
to the four of us, piled in a van
well-versed *in all four* chords,
on our way to our first gig tonight.

From a dozen people snogging in dark corners,
swaying at the bar or playing pool/darts;
to record contracts, agents, world tours
and leaving behind a trail of broken hearts.

From the dream/illusion of the road
and whistle-stop tours without a break;
to mother's cooking, clean socks
and hot water bottles bulging under covers
like rodents trapped in the bellies of snakes.

Andrew Detheridge

My Hobbies

I like when at the weekend
All the shopping's done
Then I visit friends and
We sit out in the sun

I always try the lottery
Although I never win
After I've checked my ticket
I throw it in the bin

I sometimes have a drink
When I go to bingo halls
I like trying DIY and
Hanging paper on the walls

And sometimes I settle down
To see what's on TV
But most of all I'm happy
When I'm writing poetry.

A Whyte

An Odd Pastime

'That is an odd pastime'
my prospective employer
said gingerly,
whilst scanning
my carefully put together
latest CV.
But when he'd heard
the honest detail
of my disability,
he scratched his head
and expressed his regret -
with great sincerity.

For, after careful consideration
- No! He couldn't take
a chance on me -
and what is this odd pastime?
I hear him muttering
into his tea.

Why, I've scoured for employment
for years and years -
alas, *too candidly!*

And, I scratch about,
penning this and that -
whilst, time and rhyme, pass me.

   Delia Marheineke

Pastimes . . . 'Travelling'

I have a love of travelling that transcends all other thoughts.
I've been lucky enough to see much of the world, its natural wonders,
its nature, cities and ports.

The thought of places near and far helps me through the darkest
times. Imagining the mountains, sky and sea, of fantastic foreign
climes.

I've seen the magic of the East, pondered the mysteries of
America, South.
I've sampled food in many lands, that leave tingles in the mouth!

I think Africa I love the most, the animals are myriad and sublime.
I've been to most of the countries there and I'd go back, anytime.

I love the varied cultures and peoples of this Earth
I want to absorb it more and more and appreciate it for all it's worth!

It never ceases to amaze, how diverse all countries are.
Their cultures, to each, are so unique, even though their boundries
may not be far.

I love the heat, the steaming rain, the cold . . . (I'm not too sure!)
Whatever I experience as I travel, I enjoy it more and more.

As a child of four, I watched on TV, new worlds and new sights every
day. I said to my mother I wanted to travel,
She said 'One day you *will do* as you say!'

And so it turned out, my wishes have come true.
I've been fortunate indeed to have experienced so much.
There is still much more to see and to do, I think to travel,
has been my *'life's crutch'!*

Derek J Day

On Holiday In Malta

When we had a holiday in Malta
Away from England's cold winter
We went to a place, far away
On an adventurous day

When we visited a place in Valletta
As we parked the hired car
We climbed 90 steps or so
To go to a variety show

When we came out, it rather gave us a start
As my friend and I jumped on a horse and cart
The man gave quite a frown
As we then had to climb down

The men walked along
As we followed on
One got lost on the way
It was just a disastrous day

The man who got lost, visited a shop
The other man wouldn't wait, or stop
He climbed the 90 steps or more
And nearly hit the floor

This all happened because they wouldn't part with money
For the ride on the horse and cart, for my friend and me
Just served him right
To see such a sight

The holiday was good, after all
Although he felt such a fool
But all did end well, for the holiday in Malta
Far away from old England's cold weather

Jean P McGovern

Time On My Hands?

I'm really too busy for pastimes
There are too many chores yet to do
With washing and cooking and cleaning
And presently painting the loo!
Mind - I've thirty plus pots on the patio
All packed with most beautiful flowers
And I thank them each day for their glorious display
Brought out by the sunshine and showers -
And the love that I pour on them daily
By weeding and feeding galore.
So - I really can't fit in those hobbies
They say I should start to explore.
Then - I dabble in poetry quite often
And recently published my first book.
So there hasn't been time for diversions
With all of the homework *that* took.
I organise charity concerts
Which those who attend, say are great,
And super young stars bring their dads and mammas
Who are happy to pay at the 'gate'.
I've done evening classes in Spanish
And carpentry (not very good!)
For time and again I'd murder the grain
Using more than my quota of wood
But my 'ottoman' stands there in glory
As it has for some forty-five years
Mind - not quite as long as our marriage
But it's joined in our laughter and tears.
There's always been football and cricket
Plus tennis - though now on TV
If the scores are given away before 'Match of the Day.'
I could shoot the newscaster with glee!
Then crosswords are a bit of a passion
I usually do them with meals

Having solved the last clue and checked it right thro'
How wonderfully clever I feel!
So *you'll* understand - it's nothing I've planned
It just happens that 'pastimes' aren't me
I live life the way it falls every day
Where'er I feel happy and free!
My 'sell by' date's gone - but I still soldier on
And it's now only time I can 'borrow'
Was it *pastimes* you said? Well I'm early to bed
I've got *'Beginner's Computers'* tomorrow!

And oh! By the way - I've forgotten to say
I did Hatha Yoga for years
And stood on my head, before going to bed
And full Lotus, without any fears!

But *hobbies!* At *my* age?
That's silly!
I simply just haven't the 'go'
As you'll see from the above
It's the quiet life I love
- Now - I must finish carpeting this floor!

John Elias

My Drinking Pastime

My drinking pastime, has brought pleasure and pain
A pastime to enjoy in the company of many
Yet a pastime to fill the lonely hours
When life's direction has gone off track

My drinking pastime, with book or paper
A nod of acknowledgement, a quick hello
Conversation not asked or returned
Peaceful contentment in solitude gained

My drinking pastime when laughter abounds
When friends reveal all, glass half full
Communal worries cast aside
Human spirits compliment all that's good

My drinking pastime has brought sorrow
Dreams broken, glass half empty
Solace required in a liquid fiend
Addiction pulling at my arm

My drinking pastime has cleared the air
Thoughts off the wall need fulfilling
Problems aired have brought solutions
Problem solved from the bottom of a glass

My drinking pastime between Heaven and Hell
A pastime so fine, lined crossover point
From social gathering to blabbering fool
From dancing to falling, brain cells dying

My drinking pastime is not for all
For the pain of the drink is a mighty sore
A pastime that controls and numbs and -
Cares of tomorrow can wait till this drink is done

Neil J P Phillips

Grandchildren And Other Things

Grandchildren, gardening, reading and poetry,
Pastimes I love and would never change,
Although the first two make your bones ache and creak
But the first on my list makes my life complete,
When a day doesn't go just as you planned
And things really hit rock bottom,
The simplicity of the answer is
Don't worry, we are here to give you a helping hand.
They like to help in the garden, setting bulbs and plants
I have to follow on behind
In case they put them upside down,
But when they see them start to grow
And flowers show their faces
The children's smiles and happy laughter
Makes every twinge just another chapter.

They like to read and write little verses
This quiet time we all enjoy,
They like to read the poetry I write
And tell me if they don't think it sounds right,
I make up stories to tell them each night
For they are the kings and queens of all times
I get some ideas from the stories and verses
And the children themselves are a wealth of words,
When the day is done and children asleep
Out comes my pen, my paper, and book,
I go through the day and make a few notes
Ready for the poetry to be wrote,
I pick up my book, a read before bed
But the sandman is here and lays a hand on my head,
Tomorrow is another day.

Mary Neill

A Night Out

She went to see the 'Girlfriend' at the theatre one fine day
With other ladies from the church, a cavalcade so gay
The mini bus transported them with Rusty at the wheel
His dedication to this work would demonstrate his zeal.

The music from the show was from an era long since passed
But evergreen the joy it gave could never be surpassed
The dancing, costumes, lighting, music, elegantly real
Made ladies sing and clap in time so happy did they feel.

So if you're feeling tired or sad with life's o'erwhelming load
Remember theatre when well done can take you down the road
To fantasy or fairyland or fun or tragedy
And fill your heart and mind with happy thoughts of what might be.

To lift you from the routine chores that blind you to the sun
For fleeting moments with good friends it takes us every one
For theatre is as old as time - I'm sure that this is true
So breaks from work to visit such is my advice to you.

M M Ainsworth

Walking

I like to go out walking
Whenever I have time
And as I walk I often think
That everything is fine

Walking is excellent if
You have a problem in your brain
Or if life is getting you down
And you are feeling the strain

Sometimes it is good to walk
With another person there
Somebody you like by your side
So that this view you both can share

So, if you want my opinion
I'd suggest to you
Get a friend or someone close
And take them walking too

And as you walk, you will find
Peace will warm your belly
Yes, walking in the countryside
Is better than watching telly

You don't have to go anywhere special
But, preferably, go where it's green
Go where nature is all around
And town folk can't be seen

Go there with a friend and find
Your problems disappear
As the tweeting of the birds nearby
Is the only sound you hear.

S Patterson

Greensleeves

As the man said,
Music is the food of love,
Just think what life
Would be like,
Without music,
It doesn't bear,
Thinking about,
Turn on your radio,
Or your stereo,
And nothing comes out.

Most of my spare time,
Is spent nodding,
Or toe tapping,
Along to my,
Favourite tunes,
Or sat in ancient
Auditoriums or venues,
To be enchanted,
Captivated by touring bands,
Who the motions take us through.

So all you music lovers,
Get off your backsides,
Leave your comfy armchairs,
Get out and about,
In your town,
Music abounds,
Music lives and breathes,
No matter your taste,
It's out there somewhere,
Rock, jazz, punk, blues, or if your delight is old
Greensleeves.

P J Littlefield

Gardener's Delight

It's lovely to be out in the garden.
It's lovely to be out in the fresh air.
It's lovely to behold rhododendron.
It's lovely to see result of your care.

The pleasure that you derive from seeing
The fruits of your labour in leisure,
Contributing to your health's well-being,
The benefits are far beyond measure.

Relaxing after a hard day's toil
Among the roses of various hue
The sight of well-cultivated soil,
Will surely change your mood from feeling blue.

In the evening the honeysuckle smell,
Powerful after a hot summer's day
And flowers with perfume that seems to dwell
From sunrise to sunset - a fine display.

A nation of gardeners, that we are,
Whether it's balcony, roof or box,
We'll seek the right plant from near or far,
Dutch bulbs, violets from Devon or phlox.

William Barnard

Mitcham Golfers (Or Against The Odds)

Some years ago they used to have fun
Missing the trams on the Croydon run.
Came their demise and the trolley-bus grew
To be the target of the unfortunate few,
Who sliced or hooked from the fairways green
To rattle the traffic, before, unseen.

Around the course the railway goes,
This keeps most golfers on their toes.
A slice from the fourth, you're two shots down,
A lost ball as well, no wonder you frown.
The fifth tee also, placed out on that wing,
Solicits train whistles at the top of your swing.

The West Croydon - Wimbledon line ran through,
A slice from the seventh and that was you.
But a shot from the tee as the signal went clear
Struck the raised arm giving rise to a cheer
For the ball came back and on to the green
The luckiest shot ever - believed only if seen!

Leave us alone? No, now it's Tramlink.
We've enough distractions, wouldn't you think?
But the golfer true only sees the ball
And playing this game, gives it his all.
So when he comes in to check his card
He can blame public transport for making it hard.

George Blake

Line Dance Crazy

Line dancing crazy that's my friend Joan and me
We cannot wait to finish work and get home for our tea.

And then dressed in our cowboy boots
With dresses cropped and shorn,
We rush off to the country clubs
And dance from dusk till dawn.

Dressed in our cowgirl outfits
We really look the part,
And people often comment
That we always look so smart.

Our sons say they'll disown us
If they see us in the town,
But it really does not bother us
However much they frown.

We'll carry on regardless
And continue to be tough,
Then go out to the ranch house
Or elsewhere to strut our stuff.

And for all we're in our fifties
We still strive to do our best
And be up there on the dance floor
Just to line dance like the rest.

When we're riddled with arthritis
And confined into our beds
Still our feet will keep on tapping
To the music in our heads.

Kathleen South

Send In The Clouds

Grey empty days are not for me,
They fill my soul with mis-er-y
That broods and grows, creates the foes
That smother light, that numb the brain
That steal my hopes, that bring the pain.

Yet . . . deep blue skies . . . plain, unadorned,
By watching eyes are justly scorned,
An empty canvas, nothing more,
The artist waits, his brush unsure . . .

A silence creeps across the sky,
I raise my head, begin to cry.
My voice throws sorrow in the air,
I close my eyes against the glare.

No! Open wide . . . another look!
God turns the pages of His book.
He knows I'm here, the time is now
To lift His brush, to show me how
The sky will move, will dance, will live,
The joy of life is His to give.

A white horse runs with flowing mane,
Will it ever come again?
A ship that sails on sky-blue seas,
On whitened foam, that seems to ease
The passage of the souls within
Who ride on high, rewards to win.

And now a face, benign and clear
Smiling down to calm my fear,
The Maker of these lovely clouds
Who gives me hope, removes the shrouds
That darken minds and thoughts and eyes
Who brings me to the treasured prize.

Clouds! My pictures in the sky.
My pastime for a lifetime
To study, watch, to see . . .
To have them here forever
And know the fact . . . *they're free!*

Patricia Phelan

Fifties Female Friends

From the swirling skirted sweetness
Fox-trot flavoured friendship of our youth.
Our lives never in sequence of a dance.
Like seeds we scattered and met perchance.
Branches occasionally touching on a tree.
Yet friendship has remained until maturity.
Comforting midday lunches, conversations we share.
Trust and understanding permeate the air.
Images in time, photographs hold us frozen fast.
We peel away the years with words, memories flood back.
Confide, console, confess growing old.
Elbows easy on a table rested and relaxed.

Ethel Oates

Hobbies

Putting words together
in a rambly fashion,
expressing thought and what you see and hear!
Poetry has never been so encouraging!
Reading the classics helps and hinders.
Today we are free in form and shape
whilst rhyme and timing have their place.
Each person speaks with a unique voice,
with a feel for words and sound,
pick up a pen and play with syllables
- doing a crossword in-between!

With a trowel and patio enjoying some sun,
dabbling in plants is delightful.
Pick your own herbs and flowers
and taking cuttings for fun!

Unless you try, skills remain dormant!
Pottery, usually in small friendly groups
the water-colour painting is truly therapeutic
and flower arranging a complete joy.
Rambling groups, like dancing, increase your socialising.

Margaret Ann Wheatley

The Poem That Wasn't

I dearly wanted to write a special poem
The finest to be penned, with words supreme,
Yet, no matter how long or hard I mused
I could not decide upon a suitable theme.

My trusty pen remained silent, no ink flowed
The paper stayed quite blank the whole day,
I tried, it was in vain as no ideas came
See my anger, frustration and total dismay.

All night through I deliberated, pen hovering
Attempting to create that one opening line,
No inspiration materialised inside my head
My poetic days are over, on the decline.

The following morning continued unchanged
A day's stubble now shadowed my chin,
I wracked my brain from inside and out
Nothing there, just like an empty coffee tin.

After a week I had made zero progress
The only words on the sheet, Basildon Bond,
I had not eaten, drank or showered
In fact I looked akin to a vagabond.

One month later I was still contemplating
Now a complete zombie, could I but scream,
Then suddenly the end came to my dilemma
I woke up, it was only a horrible dream.

George S Johnstone

The Golfer

I 'wanna-be' a golfer with a handicap of three ~
then I could join the conversation with great authority,
I'd tell of driving at the fourth and landing near the pin,
how birdies never came my way ~ one stopped this going in.

At the sixth ~ an easy par four ~ I nearly did the same
in two I landed on the green, I'm doing well this game;
this started off an eagle, then a birdie, then a par ~
then a gust of wind got under it and hit a passing car.

I par'd the eighth quite easily, but the bunker on the tenth ~
grew bigger every second in depth and width and length;
the next hole was a short one, it should have gone straight in
but the ball stayed nestled on the tee and the divot hit the pin.

There are putters, woods and irons ~ do I use a seven or eight?
I'll flick some grass into the wind to help decide my fate.
With rules and regulations that turn good friends into foes ~
I'll stay indoors, drink vintage port and train for dominoes.

Jim Pritchard

Pastimes

My favourite pastimes - poetry and gin,
Surely that can't be a sin!
Nothing wrong with such pleasures,
Both I do - at my leisure!

I also like to take a walk,
With a friend - so we may talk!
Whilst admiring the flora all around,
And stopping to listen to every sound!

I often go out on my bike,
Equally as pleasant as a hike!
The difference is - I rest my feet,
When walking - I feel I'm on the beat!

Collecting pebbles on the shore,
And picking blackberries by the score!
Chopping wood - then watching it burn,
Potting up the garden urn!

Outdoor pursuits - I love the best,
Then enjoying my gin - when it's time to rest!
Time to reflect on my favourite pastime,
Bring happy thoughts - and words that rhyme!

Carol Edney

Melior

Looking out across towards the sea,
Seeing the beauty of it all and feeling free.
Steam trains stood still, for they no longer run,
Shining in the sunlight bright as new.
History surrounds this tiny place,
Lost from the world; time and space.
The green of the grass next to the coal,
Atmosphere builds and warms the soul.
Melior lies waiting in her shed,
Waiting for her fire to be lit burning yellow and red.
Her steam builds up; the smoke turns white from black,
Before she speeds up, as she rolls down the track.
Open her throttle and set her free,
As she runs past bushes, lakes and trees.
Tooting the whistle to reduce the steam,
People stare, their faces beam.
Back to her shed to let her cool down,
Then we leave this place and go back to town.

A M Williamson

Books

Books, how I love them,
on tall shelves piled high.
Old books and new books, I love them all,
hardbacks and paperbacks, how some make me cry.
Clean books and dusty books, large print and small,
some only just published in new shiny jackets,
or leather-bound shabby old and well worn.
Books whose authors are obscure or well known.
I read every night at dusk and at dawn.
Fiction, non fiction, biographies too,
adventure, murder, sci fi, all these I read.
I read when I am travelling, or when I am alone,
I ignore the neighbours, the doorbell, the 'phone.
Please leave me alone with my books I plead.
I am really so happy, when I start to read.
Books I have everywhere, thousands I know,
piled up in the kitchen, the bedroom, the hall.
You may call me eccentric, of that I am sure,
but when I sit in my old rocking chair,
a glass of wine, a good book
who could really ask for more?

Dorothy Chadwick

Biker's Dream

Why man I had to build a machine,
A bike this world had never seen.
Speed, that no man can catch my ass,
They just know something's gone, as I fly past!

Chrome, like mirrors that catch the light,
A dazzle that appears, then gone, what a fright.
Well I have found the magic of speed,
Plus have the meanest machine, that's greed!

As I roar into town they stand and stare,
But no man touches, they wouldn't dare!
Speed cameras flash but they can't say,
For I'm gone, how I like to play.

No machine can touch its class,
So when you see a flash, watch your ass!

Ann Beard

Woodturning

Fashioned of spirit and light
The heart of the tree
Encased in deadwood
Retains its dignity and reveals
Its inner secrets
Spalded ribs, sapwood, heart
Respond to the gentle touch
As form, shape and beauty
Emerges to salute a new life
In a whirlpool of energy
To honour its Creator.

Una Sheeran

Annual Exhibition

An art exhibition in a hall or place
Which has a large room and given space
To artists devoting hours to create.
At the weekend, at times in the day,
View the inspirational display
Please make a note of the date.
Water-colour, pastel and oil
Attention is given to each frame
Worthy results of the time and toil
Each has a title and owner's name.
Mind absorbed in a local view
Garden, still-life or zoo
Portrait of a mysterious face
Reclining figure in lace
Memories of a holiday
A building, flower or picturesque bay.
It is appreciated to share
Works unique and rare,
People view without a sound
As each takes a last glimpse round.

Sylvia Berwick

Have A Good Read

If you want to relax
and at life take a look,
why not curl up
and enjoy a good book.

You learn such a lot
from the stories they tell.
Adventure, love and courage,
and lots more as well.

They teach about life
and how to cook.
So why don't you
curl up with a book?

Julie Brown

Pastimes

What is it that makes me think
That I can write poetry in a blink

And scoff the Muse, who says to me:
'I can't inspire you - so let it be?'

I'll try to endow you with the grace to dance,
Or fling yourself merrily into a trance;

Perhaps you would like to become quite witty,
With a latent penchant for singing a 'ditty'?

But, just as I feel compelled to believe
The timely warning, which I receive -

Out of the blue, there comes a calling
And into a stupor I find myself falling

Of turns of phrase and publishers' blurb
That really makes me feel quite absurd:

Would you imagine that the writing of a Keats or Shelley
Could cause me to be involved in such a mêlée?

Yet still I long to pick up the pen
And follow in the footsteps of such men,

Who strove to go beyond the mundane
And enrich the world with so much gain -

Of aerial view, or classical theme,
To wean mankind from that which is mean.

Yes, I'll still continue to struggle and write my verse,
And hope that it never becomes a curse.

Bernadette Marley

Nature's Miracle

I look out at my garden bare
Ravaged by winter's wind unfair,
Where is spring with its brightest flowers?
I long for warming sunny hours
And time to spend with nature's care
To create a show not yet there.

There's work to do, no time to rest,
These are the days that really test
Endurance and dedication,
Result then, a fine creation
Exciting show of summer flowers
That please the eye for hours and hours.

Now the saddened bedraggled lawn
Looked down upon by trees with scorn,
Would seem to say with tiresome plea
'Shine down warm sun and rescue me,'
As if those words are really heard
The sun appears with song of bird.

And now the work is here at hand,
The time is right for days well planned,
As days go by we see the start
Nature's creation cheers the heart
And we marvel with sheer delight
All on show, a beautiful sight.

The bright array of summer shades,
Enchanting lawns of verdant blades,
A scene of pleasure soothes the eye
With peace that calms bringing great joy,
Relaxed emotions now with ease
Feelings so good that really please.

Compliments to a job well done,
Sweet roundelays in the warming sun.

Irene Grahame

The Blues Boy
(For Michael)

A droplet in a restless ocean of blue and white,
she searches hopefully for his face
lost to her this Saturday afternoon
on the far-reaching television screen.

Streams of chanting spill over the stadium
and the deep, fierce heartbeat of the crowd throbs.
Somewhere in the waves of curses and swearing
he stands firm as a small, clear rock
with a furrowed brow focus on the tide of the game,
noting every surge of the players, every dive.
Woollen hat pulled well down and thick, nearly choking scarf,
he smiles only when his team scores.
A Mars bar melting in his hand, as he dreams
he is a captain or a goalie in the net.
Magnetised by the ball's flow, bodies ripple and swell as one,
until the long jet of the final whistle blows.
Then a gradual ebb of supporters from the stands
as they flood homewards in the damp, darkening streets.

She switches off shared moments, starts to prepare his meal,
and the game's highlights for evening discussion.
Fish and chips for a win, a draw.
For a defeat, something extra special.

Helen Dalgleish

Pastimes

A pastime is a camera, an accessory in fact.
Through the changing seasons, always at the ready,
Capturing a fleeting scene, in the blink of an eye,
With a swift click of the shutter, the hands held steady.

A cool orb in a winter's glassy sky
Glints on the crystal flakes of snowy nap.
Dark boughs, bare, stretch to the heavens;
All this permanently imaged in a moment's snap.

To enfold the rich colours of spring,
Or a misty lake, illuminating the sun.
The bursting of greens in forest and hedge
Is satisfaction indeed as the frames roll one by one.

High summer's action with outdoor pursuits
Bring many chance shots of lively stance.
Splendid panoramas of distant views
Are caught on film as is a local country dance.

Incentive, no doubt, is to record through the lens
Russets of autumn, the reds and the gold.
First frosts that coldly cover all in their path,
A year's passing pageant, to forever behold.

Lizbeth Cooke

The Brewers Of Faversham

To the brewers of Faversham,
kindly lend me your ear,
just a moment of your time,
to think on good English beer.

Old Thumper and Old Peculier,
to begin by naming two,
right and worthy entries,
in my good beer 'Who's Who'.

Abbot Ale and Ruddles County,
even Bishops Tipple when found,
three cask conditioned ales,
of character and noble renown.

From noble ales to royal ales,
and then to pints heaven sent,
Spitfire and Bishops Finger,
my pilgrimage takes me to Kent.

Christmas ale with cherry brandy,
and the oldest brewery in the land,
I raise my glass in toast,
to celebrate the finest ale to hand.

In praise of all at Shepherd Neame,
master brewers both present and old,
I send you millennium good cheer,
and open my first bottle of Kent-Gold.

Keith Leese

Treasure

Have you ever noticed how little children play?
So deep in thought with very little to say.
As I walk through wet sand, gentle waves wash my feet;
A child splashes forward and then retreats.

The water is cool as it reaches his toes ~ soon
down on his knees his enthusiasm grows.
Close by a treasure brought in by the sea.
Small hands reach out, what can it be?

Standing by quietly, I watch and smile.
What treasure has been found in the soft wet mound.
It's a green shiny bottle that's causing delight.
I wonder, will he take it home, or float it out of sight,
enclosing a message from someone far away,
over the distant ocean, treasure for another day.

The words may relate God's love and devotion.
How vast His creation and all He has made.
Treasure indeed that will never ever fade.
The green shiny bottle bobs slowly out of sight.
Where next will it rest, will it tell of God's might?

Jean Jackson

Now Look Here

My life is all pastime, I no longer go to work
It doesn't mean I sit around all day and shirk
Nor do I lay in bed all day or sit watching the telly
I have to go shopping for food to feed my belly

I have an early morning walk beside the rolling sea
Photographs of the rising sun for many folks to see
Photography is my hobby, I try not other people to bore
And in our club competitions I've won a score or more

I've took many thousands of photos to this very day
I hope to take thousands more before I pass away
For over fifty years I have enjoyed my hobby
Now just hang on a minute while I photograph a bobby

Besides taking sunrise, sunsets and still-life
I've tried my hand at action shots and wildlife
I've taken photos in the garden, roses in full boom
Also photographs at weddings, especially the bride and groom

I clean my rooms, I dig the garden, I cut the lawn
I trim the hedge, I'm up at the crack of dawn
I wash and iron and write poetry when I can
But I love going out with a camera in my hand

Harry Skinn

Pleasure

Nothing can be more relaxing,
than to sit on the River Brew.
Hearing the first songbird sing,
and the grass all covered in dew.

The trout rising to a hatch of flies,
is a wonderful sight to see.
And when you finally hook in one,
you tremble at the knees.

Away from all the busy streets,
and the trouble that they bring.
There's nothing here to harm you,
just nature enjoying spring.

It seems to me like another world,
and so far from all life's pain.
The only temptation that exists,
is to return tomorrow again.

No one can take this from me,
it's a love within my heart.
I'll come each day to enjoy it,
until this life I do depart.

This is my Heaven and my Earth,
my morning, day and night.
So if I'm only dreaming,
let me sleep until daylight.

Nigel Quinn

I Love A Piano

At 11, keyboard lessons were my desire,
Radio pianists having set my dreams on fire.
I aimed to do a passable imitation
Until I faced practice and all its frustration.
Two teachers, one young and one old, fell to my lot,
But both were at one in thinking me not so hot.
Teenaged Olive Coleman scorned my musical choice,
But old Flora Dixon was moderate of voice.
Her mature help guided me through many a test,
Although her taste in pieces did reduce my zest.
Also, my home piano was old, stiff and slow,
Which made for performances which just didn't flow.
So, despite knowing it was the excuse of fools,
Like a poor workman, I started blaming my tools.
Yet, if my prowess could be put in a thimble,
At least all the effort kept my fingers nimble.
Now, when I can play only half as well as then,
My hands are still as supple as they were at 10.

Allan Bula

128

A Special Gift

An expression of the soul in verse,
An instrument of God
To speak of wonders, feelings, sights,
And where Christ's feet have trod
To lead along the pathways
Life's journey brings along -
And praise Him for this gift to write
Thro' poetry and song.

My heart speaks out the message He gives,
My pen His tool in hand
To tell of creation, emotions, life,
Each as I'm shown to understand
By learning thro' my lifetime
The ups and downs it brings,
And sense His presence thro' each day -
From whence my poetry springs.

Words may flow and my senses reel -
Experiences from within
Speak of things *He* needs to say
And thus attention win
To teach the world what man has done
By the spoiling of God's world -
And teach God's love that all may share
His love thro' Christ unfurled.

Ann Voaden

Dancing For Joy

We thought we would take up dancing
It looked a lot of fun
A way of getting out, and meeting everyone
So we put our best foot forward
The wrong one, no doubt
We stepped on each other's toes, he gave a shout
We must start having lessons
It is just not good enough
A course of one hour lessons
To get us round the floor
But when we got together it seemed to cause uproar
Our teacher suffered with us, all without complaint
There is no doubt about it, she really is a saint
She showed us how to keep together avoiding each other's feet
We managed to get it right, and stay upon the beat
There really is much more to this than meets the eye
We'll get this fox-trot right, if it takes until we die
So with determination we dance around the floor
Somehow, it just gets to you
You crave it more and more
So if you want something to do
Why not come and join us
You might like it too.

Rosemarie Wilkinson

Pastimes

I have a lovely garden with bushes, lawns and trees
I sit outside in summer fanned by a gentle breeze.
The dark clouds come over and shut out all the sun
And I remember vaguely that housework should be done.
So I get out my electric sweeper and plug it in the hall
Then the phone rings out, a pal in trouble makes an urgent call.
So I sit and chat and tell her all my family news
And manage to clear away her nasty fit of blues.
Then another friend calls round and we put up our tennis net,
The first ball that is hit you can make a certain bet
Will land in next door's garden and we have to knock their door.
'Please can we have our ball back? We won't do it any more!'
We are both over eighty and feel very proud to say
We can still enjoy a game and hope that, come what may,
We continue to face our life ahead with laughter and with fun
And when we pray we both will say, 'Thy will be done.'
We don't wish to boast but we live contented lives,
We know there is a God above and when the time arrives
For us to leave this earthly home and go to Heaven's Door
We'll meet all the lovely friends who have gone before.

Inez M Henson

Fisherman's Tale

I wished to take up bear-baiting -
I even bought a bear.
I hooked it on my fishing line.
It didn't turn a hair.

I lugged it to the riverside,
Plonked in an old wheelbarrow.
The river at that point was deep,
Precipitous and narrow.

Over rugged rocks the rapids roared,
A raging water feature.
I cast my line baited with bear,
It drowned, the silly creature.

The moral of this story is:
If you would bait a bruin,
Make sure that it can swim or else
It's tantamount to ruin.

Adhering to a hook, for bears,
Is hard, it must be said.
So, if you wish to catch a fish,
Try using worms instead.

Norman Bissett

Chess

Place in place,
The wooden
Pieces bristle
In rank and file.

Face to face,
All ardent then
Waiting
For despatches,
The armies stall.

Nicola Barnes

Words Are Just Words

Sit down with an idea
Hoping to make it clear
But words are just words from the mind
Nothing is sure within my time

Looking at the world we see
Knowing how we want to be
But words are just words and that's OK
Words are just words we're on our way

We write the songs for you
Do you ever wonder why
We write the songs for you
And the words don't lie
No the words don't lie

Where do we come from
Buried in our songs
But words are just words in my imagination
Ideas come from my interpretation for you

We write the songs for you
Do you ever wonder why
We write the songs for you
And the words don't lie
No the words don't lie

J Cook

Writer's Confession

The pen is a deadly weapon
To be used in any season
And for any reason.
For murder, for love, for treason.
What you write, will have effect,
So be careful and protect.
Many writers write to make a point.
They come across as something they ain't.
Sometimes we go too far.
We think we're some kind of superstar
But I write from the heart.
My stories play a part.
If you read them it's a start.
If you believe in them I fear your heart.

Laura Sansom

Contentment

He was an industrialist of repute, affluent by far,
Leisure he had a'plenty, to meander near and far,
Rambled he on a holiday, south of his home border,
To study human nature, in the guise of an explorer!
Strolling along the beach where palm trees swayed from side to side,
He stopped, startled at the spectre, which him had horrified!
He saw a fat fisherman smoking his pipe with delight,
Reclining on his fishing boat, with his long legs astride.
Said he to the nonchalant sleepy fisherman, 'Good day . . .
Hi mate! Why aren't you out fishing on this very nice day?'
Quipped the fisherman quite indifferently and bluntly,
'Because I have caught enough fish today already.'
'Why don't you catch more than you need?' asked the industrialist.
Replied the fisherman - 'What on Earth would I do with it?'
Pondered the industrialist - 'You could earn more money,
You could then buy a motor to make your boat ply more swiftly;
Then you could go into deeper waters by day and night,
Catch more fish, earn more money, buy nylon nets, taut and tight,
Perhaps, even buy a fleet of boats, or flotilla, maybe,
Culminating in becoming a very rich man like me!'
The fisherman pondered nonplussed, and thoughtfully answered,
'What Sir, would I do then?' He sighed mournfully and nodded;
'Then you could sit down and enjoy life very peacefully!'
Taken aback, the fisherman replied nonchalantly,
'What do you think I'm doing right now? You silly Billy!'

Welch Jeyaraj Balasingam

Gardeners' Petitions

Preserve the roses from greenfly -
oh, may the compost rot!
Deliver all nasturtiums
from scourge of the Black Spot.
Shrivel the root of every weed
and tame each wayward plot.

Let water hoses not be banned
if days turn very warm.
May plastic tubs and fluted urns
reveal a hidden charm.
Let slug bait do its worthy work
yet cause our pets no harm.

Now help us all to persevere
and learn the way to bend
that we become more rugged yet
when joints begin to mend.
We do not covet Chelsea's gold,
but oh - greenfingers send!

Margaret Connor

Sign Language

I went to learn sign language
In Bangor tech' one day
After the introduction
I wasn't sure if I would stay

The tutor, he was very nice
The class members, they were too
The booklet I was handed
Showed I had a lot to do

First I learnt the alphabet
It was hard enough to do
My fingers got all muddled up
I really had no clue

But as the weeks went by
I picked things up quite fast
I was able to communicate
I was learning it at last

Sometimes I did get nervous
When I was asked to sign
But I always liked to have a go
Most times things turned out fine

Soon I could tell short stories
And hold a conversation too
I could understand the tutor
Which at first was hard to do

I felt that I achieved a lot
Much more than I expected
And when I signed to Stephen
My efforts were respected

I'm glad I learnt sign language
And although it's just stage one
I feel I have the confidence
to sign to anyone

J L Preston

Pastimes

Many are the hobbies I have known throughout the years,
Some have brought me pleasure, others would end in tears.
When I was a little girl a box of paints would do,
But as I grew older much more I wanted too.
Schoolfriends and I together, we just tried them all,
Skipping, jumping, hopscotch, playing with a ball.
Tried many collections, tired of the lot,
Mum and Dad got fed up paying for all we got.
I tried playing tennis but proved no good at that.
Dad said I'd be better to lose some of my fat.
What I didn't understand they'd been through this too,
Realised it would take time for me to see it through.
Looking back along the years I really have to smile,
Because I was so full of me it really took a while
To see I really was enjoying these experiments,
Then I got a boyfriend, a natty little gent,
He now is my husband, we have kids of our own.
We are both awaiting until they are full grown,
This is when the lot of them then will understand,
The hobbies of the days now past, are at their command,
Which has shown them how to live, faithful, fond and true,
Good citizens within this world just as we taught them to.

Barbara Goode

Basketball Fever

The lights go down,
The line-ups are called,
Court-side atmosphere is electric,
The players encircle on the floor.

Their skills and game on the line,
Ready to play, ready for the ball to be tipped,
Let's get ready to rumble!
The ball goes to one player.

He's up for the challenge ahead,
This is going to get physical,
Hope you don't slip! Hope you don't fall!
He sets his pick, he makes his drive,
The hoop awaits, got to get the points to survive.

Fake it this way, shake it and then bake it,
Whichever way you jam the ball,
Either a long range three pointer,
A swish jump shot or with finesse
See the hangtime, the agility and beauty in the motion,
Is it in the juice? No! It's pure emotion.

When he slams it down with authority
The fans get up on their feet with admiration,
They show the deserved applause
For how much heart and sweat he's given -
The team power on,
Many snap decisions go this way and that,
This is basketball fever,
Take it all the way, you know you can!

Matthew Lindley

Two Oceans Marathon Capetown

An early start and it's still dark
There's a buzz in the crowd and excitement too
As the day I've been waiting for has finally come through.

All the training done through weather both fair and rough
With friends by my side to help me through the tough
Now I am on my own and the gun sets the start.
With thirty-five miles to run I run with all my heart
And try to have fun for there's a medal to be won.

The cheers and applause ring in my ears
With eight thousand runners
It feels like I am the only one here.

Remember the training, don't go off too fast
Go steady and enjoy the views
Table Mountain is a sight to see
Breathtaking scenes it seems like a dream.

Five hours and thirty-two minutes later I cross the line
Singing, 'She'll be coming round the mountain when she comes.'
A bronze medal I am proud to wear, I've done it, I'm fine.

Colleen Nealon

Our Pastimes

My pastime is fascinating and means a lot to me
I'm organising photographs as 'Creative Memories'.
From my early days of childhood, to grandchildren, present time,
I'm placing them in albums with a thought, or verse or rhyme.

Then I add some stickers, or a coloured cut out shape
Using attractive scissors, fixing with special tape.
I have templates that make circles, ovals, shapes and wavy lines
The pages are all 'acid free' and protected for all time.

I often trim some photographs, known as 'cropping' them
Or use my 'corner rounder', subjects look better then.
My albums bring great pleasure to my family and me
Each page provides forever a 'Creative Memory'.

My husband enjoyed gardening, along with DIY
He made marquetry pictures, crossword puzzles he would try.
He also read a lot of books and Scrabble used to play
But something's taken over to take his time away.

He sits for many an hour gazing in the face
Of his new shining monster that has taken up our space.
His expression is perplexed for he does not understand
Information fed to him by a 'mouse' held in his hand.

The clicking and the flicking is enough to give headaches,
Or bring eyestrain, unless one quickly spots mistakes.
One hears all day of floppy discs, memory and CD ROM
The world-wide web and Internet, yet it's still not played 'our song'.

I really wish that lessons he'd take, or find a tutor
For he's bewitched by 'Windows' within his new computer.
He's determined he will beat it, the monster's mind is greater
For it's storing information, perhaps sooner or later

When the novelty has worn, and 'Big Brother's' left alone
Maybe then I'll have the chance to 'crash' him on my own . . .

Joan Heybourn

Fred

It is supposed a gardener goes
About his jobs with bent intent,
To plant his seed in perfect rows
And win the cup at the annual event.

He's always looking to the sky
And tries to study whether,
He must always supply the WI,
Him and Jim together.

He goes to the beaches to get bags of kelp,
He does it all without any help.
He goes to the quarry to get some lime,
Which takes up at awful lot of time.

The manure is there for all to share,
So as soon as it is dawning
Fred is quick to take the lot,
While the other folk are yawning.

This task takes all year long,
While others have a rest,
They start in March when the weather's good,
And they still come out the best.

In spring his garden looks a sight,
There's none that can compare.
Tending seedlings day and night.
With little time to spare.

Off to the library at post-haste,
For to learn from a book.
With very little time to waste,
He has vegetables to cook.

Summer time Fred takes his ease,
His garden now complete:
But there's sparrows now amongst the peas,
So get up off your seat.

F J Simpson

The Allotment

Black earth, enriched with compost and loam,
Old kitchen waste, smelly product of home,
Fertiliser, lime, with phosphate and dung,
Attacking with glee, throat, nostril and lung.

Pouring o'er catalogues, illustrating seed,
Artfully tempting your desperate need
To go one better than t'other bloke's plot,
By selecting what you think is best of the lot.

Carefully sowing when weather's just right,
Got to make sure there's no frost at night,
Covering with net to foil hungry birds
With youngsters to feed, oblivious to words.

Tending the young plants and chopping down weeds
That spring up remorselessly, choking your seeds,
Watering the roots when it's so hot and dry,
Recalling the days you were so young and spry.

Then comes the autumn, you're ready to drop,
But looking with pride at a wonderful crop,
Your wrinkled old face breaking into a smile,
And you say to yourself, 'By God, it's worthwhile.'

G K (Bill) Baker

Part-Time Poet

For me poetry writing is fun
We all know how it's done
Playing with words, great for the brain
The power of thought to train.

Oh! Tear it up and start again.

To get those words in some order
Conveying a story, a message, a thought
It's a challenge not to be missed
Up there with that first kiss.

No, tear it up and start again.

So there you have it
Getting the message across
Requires poetic words, not dross
Like what's written here.

Awful, try again later dear.

Now let me have a go.

'Today I saw a little worm
Wriggling on his belly
Perhaps he'd like to come inside
And see what's on the telly.'

OK . . . you clever Joe.

Richard Phillips

Pastimes

Pastimes - oh what fun they were,
    jumping becks and swinging high in the air
walking for miles and sitting with sighs
    watching those cotton wool clouds float by.

Then as years passed and children came
    no time then for those pastimes
The world changes idiom and starts a pace
    to do better and better in life's race.

Time take up with knitting and sewing
    washing and ironing all to keep going
football and cricket, sword dancing too
    all went to put us in a fine stew.

All years have gone, it's the end of the line
    time yet again for all those pastimes
so, off you go to your dancing - what bliss!
    'Til along comes to you, a baby's first kiss.

Back we go to the old mundane things
    that made our hearts happy and gave us new wings,
there's so many pastimes when love is around.

    Beth Spinks

DIY Man

This 'Do-It-Yourself' thing is all very well,
And a whole generation's hard at it - pell mell!
They work every moment from morning till bed,
And they wouldn't stop them if they weren't half dead!

With a box full of tools, and a few scribbled plans,
They tackle blocked manholes and lavatory pans.
They'll attend to the plumbing and love laying bricks -
But I think it's the noise which provides them with kicks!

They plug in the drill or the circular saw,
And then they're away on a trip without flaw.
The whine of the jigsaw as timber they cut
Is music from Heaven to the DIY nut!

Now, painting is boring, for using a brush
Produces no racket, or not very much.
But just think of the thrill a big hammer can cause
When applied with unending and deafening force!

Now the DIY man's in a world set apart
As he hammers and saws, and pursues his odd art.
Does he ever, I wonder, give thought to the stress
That he causes in others as he clears up his mess?

It's ironic to think that this 'hobby' began
To conserve the finances of DIY Man.
But now it's become a great passion, so strong
And he's got so obsessed that he goes on too long.

So his family, neighbours, and his very best friend
Get tired very soon of his toil without end,
And the outcome may be that, his welcome outstayed,
He'll have to go back to the craftsman who's paid!

Angus MacDonald

Hobbies

There isn't a hobby I can't do, if I really try.
I may be over sixty but I'm still rather spry.
Design and making dolls houses is something I enjoy.
Design and making dolls for girl or boy.
Crocheting blankets for the charity shop.
Making pots on a wheel that never seems to stop.
Lace making is not a chore.
Book reading is something I really do adore.
My spinning wheel is upstairs waiting for another fleece.
My weaving loom is also there lying in peace.
Embroidery and tapestry, and rag rug making too.
With all I have before me, I don't have time to be blue.
Now I won't have time to play,
I have to finish this poem for Poetry Today.

Zoe French

Sweet William - Filling The Bill

'Sweet William', delicious frilly napkin, sumptuous spring juicy
                                          jujube frolicking
Serving servitude to a molasses mash, to unprovoked winter hash
Stew pot of unruly thought, dissembling critic of biennial trash

True grit of courage to stay put and fast, until the roses bloom at last
Don't give up hope because it's time for bed
Soon again to raise your head; giving back the lie
To greying clouding dreary sky

We know you'll come and not look back
At scudding rain and snows attack
Companion of my giddy Easter feast
Coloured blessing round my feet

Pluto

Line Dancing

We are learning how to line dance. It seemed quite hard at first.
Some steps we do have funny names, like 'Coaster Step' and worse!

One that's called a 'Twinkle' and another, 'Kick - Ball - Chain.'
All the dances that we learn, there's never two the same.

We like the dance we call 'Ooo! Aah!' and one called 'Smoky Places'.
There's 'Sleazy Slide', 'Mucara Walk' and another is 'Country Races'.

Our teacher's name is Gregory. Greg we say for short.
He has a lot of patience; far more than he ought.

Each week we go through all the steps that we have done before.
We do half turns; and some full turns; until he thinks we're sure.

When everyone has grasped it; he plays the music slow,
Then, faster - faster - faster - until it starts to flow.

They really are such fun to do; until we fail to see,
That when the dance is ended, we are - not - where we should be.

Molly Phasey

Postcards From Iona

When I was four years old he brought us gifts -
Sweets from Iona and
A wee birdbath, worked by hand,
Mirroring both sea and sand.

Trapped sunlight sparkled in its sandstone bowl -
A wagtail's diving school,
Finch's font or swimming pool,
Keeping tomtits spruce and cool.

Iona was to me, at four, a place
Unknown, a mystery,
A dream, wafting history
Landwards to my chum and me.

Those were the days of sugar rationing -
Coupons for liquorice,
He the bearer from the west
Of gifts from the Eucharist,

Combining sandstone, sunlight, sweetness, sea.
Two decades passed me by,
A city-dweller. Davey
Fell ill, doomed, they said, to die

From silicosis, lungs black as the pit,
Losing all will to live.
But Iona's redemptive.
Pilgrim, seeker, fugitive,

I followed in the footsteps of the dove.
Six postcards conquered death,
Wafted to him living breath
Glorious as any birdbath.

Interdependency of sand and sea,
Proclaiming immortality.

Faith Bissett

153

Pastimes

Pastimes for me, are a thing of the past,
I am disabled, with a heart condition, how long will I last?

However, my memories of enjoying badminton, golf and tennis,
Are with me forever and in all these sports, I was quite a menace.

You look back to the days, when you were fit,
Now alas, you take life bit by bit.

   Colin Fraser

Words

No one denies the power of words
As they bring on a smile, a laugh or a tear.
One word makes our greatest fear seem absurd,
Another sounds a chord we've been longing to hear.

But how can I say what I want you to see
As I fumble with words that seem so cliched?
How will you know what you mean to me
If inspiration deserts me, and semantics evade?

I need words that stroke and caress and invite,
Gentle words that enfold you into my arms.
Give me words to entice, to touch, to excite.
Give me meanings to aid me and help to disarm.

For you are my life, my heart and my soul.
Dancing, entwining, our love ever grows.
If I stand apart your touch leads me home,
So when life intrudes, see my words, and know.

Sharon Mary Birch

Eluding All

Momentary blissfulness
The like I have not seen
Among the lasting segments
Of all that went between
Creating golden moments
Of what did go before
The end and the beginning
Eluding all once more.

A E Jones

The Magic Of Bridge

Years ago I heard a wise friend say,
'The game of bridge you must learn to play'.
She gave me some lessons and I tried so hard
To master the game, card by card.

I learned to shuffle and cut and deal,
But my lack of knowledge I couldn't conceal
When one fearful day to the bridge club I crept
But the members were so kind - I could have wept!

They told me to practise and persevere
And I gradually improved, year by year.
I bought books and videos and started to cram
Then the thrill of success when I made a 'Grand Slam'!

I've had so much pleasure and joy from the game
And made many friends - they would be hard to name!
We have lots of bridge lunches, teas and dinners
And charity days with prizes for the winners.

Bridge is a life-line to the lonely and housebound
For the more adventurous-cruises abound.
Learning to play bridge I'll never regret.
The wise words of my friend I won't forget.

Pauline M Shuttle

A Well Read Book

It's never too late, at any age
To turn and start, a brand new page.
If all the words, have all been said
If all the pages, have been read,
Open your eyes, and take a look
Take from the shelf, an unread book.

For whether it's novel, love story or spy
If all the pages are yellowed and dry
No smiles left, let alone a laugh
You know what's in each paragraph.
If the words no longer are sinking in,
Then put it down, don't even begin.

Give it away, perhaps to a friend
You'll not finish the chapter, let alone the end
No need for a bookmark to keep the place
It's written, all over your worried face.
Don't forget, as you walk out the door
The library's full of many more.

Carol Mogford

Arborist?

Have made a little arbor, hope it won't be a flop
And the four fruit trees grow up it to the tit-box on the top.
Thought of a runway of arbor lights to encourage the tits in flight
Doubt if they'll tell them anything for they won't fly at night.
The mind then turns to fairy lights, maybe I am out of my wits
Could get one or the other, perhaps both, fairies and tits.
Wondered about politics, what colour to paint the pipes
Should it be red, white, blue and orange or just blue and
yellow in stripes?
Decided they would be, like the majority, self survival it
always has been
So mixed all the colours together, came up with a dirty green.
The pipes have been used for various things, seem to mature with age
Whatever next one wonders, make a good monkey cage
With two old tyres on the heap, wire netting 'neath the dustbin lids
Failing to purchase two monkeys, can always call on the kids.
With the ramblings of the mind have tried to get this down in rhyme
For to call myself a poet would only be a crime
Can call myself a plumber, that I know I should
Can't say I'm a chippy as I only play with wood
Have dabbled as a bricky, so amongst my growing list
If all the trees grow up the poles, will I be an arborist?

Cliff Wilson

Good Money

An antique dealer
Said of another,
'Off him you'll
Only get eight.'

'Deal with me,
And I'll give
You three.'
(If you're lucky mate!)

Ian Stephenson

Doddle

It's supposed to be as easy as a-b-c.

You sit at your desk, sort out
paper and pens and hey presto!
Off you go, everything flows.
Ideas and words blow
across the paper, magnetised
to the right shapes like
verbally spun iron pyrites,
and, at the end of the day
what you wanted to say
lines up like a regiment
                    of
                    sentiment,
clearly stated as any
'sounding brass or tinkling cymbal'.

But it's not like that.
You see, I've grown to know
how terrifying, difficult,
simplicity can be.

Jim Rogerson